Swift Internals

A Deep Dive into the Compiler, Concurrency, and Architecture

by Aaqib Hussain

Swift Internals

Aaqib Hussain

Notice of Rights

Notice of Liability

Trademarks

ISBN: 978-1-950325-98-6

Table of Contents

Book License

Before You Begin

This section tells you a few things you need to know before you get started, such as what you'll need for hardware and software, where to find the project files for this book, and more.

What You Need

To follow along with this book, you'll need the following:

- **A Mac running macOS Tahoe or later.** with the latest point release and security patches installed. This is so you can install the latest version of the required development tool: Xcode.
- **Xcode 16 or later.** Xcode is the main development tool for writing code in Swift. You can download the latest version of Xcode for free from the Mac App Store, here: apple.co/1FLn51R

If you haven't installed the latest version of Xcode, be sure to do that before continuing with the book.

Book Source Code & Forums

Where to Download the Materials for This Book

The materials for this book can be cloned or downloaded from the GitHub book materials repository:

- https://github.com/kodecocodes/sme-materials/tree/editions/1.0

Forums

We've also set up an official forum for the book at https://forums.kodeco.com/c/books/swift-internals. This is a great place to ask questions about the book or to submit any errors you may find.

"This book is dedicated to my family. A special thanks to my mother, father, and sister, whose constant support and persistent questions about my progress may have annoyed me at times but ultimately kept me on schedule. And to my daughter. This book is for you.To those who challenged me to be a better engineer: this wouldn't have been possible without your guidance. Many thanks to the team at Kodeco (http://kodeco.com/) and everyone involved in this book."

— Aaqib Hussain

About the Author

Aaqib Hussain is an iOS Engineer who has been living and breathing Swift since its first release. With over a decade of experience, he has navigated every migration from Swift 1 to modern concurrency. A frequent contributor to Kodeco, Aaqib loves deconstructing the language's evolution and teaching others how it works. When he isn't at the keyboard, you can find him bowling, exploring new cuisines, doing photography, or traveling.

About the Editor

Prajwal S Belagavi is the final pass editor of this book. He resides in Bengaluru, India, and is an MBA graduate working at a leading credit card company. His interests span Swift, Android, Flutter, DeepTech, and Finance. He's a big time foodie, exploring breakfast places in Bengaluru. He loves trekking and flying his drone, and occasionally creates reels.

Introduction

Welcome to the First Edition of Swift Internals. This book explores the internal systems that make Swift work, going beyond syntax to understand the dynamics behind the language.

Over the last decade, Swift has gone from a secret project at Apple, Inc. to a full-blown, open-source, community-driven language. It continues to refine its core goal of being a general-purpose language that supports safety, speed and expressiveness.

Most developers learn Swift by building features, but the deeper mechanisms of the language often remain hidden. Understanding how the compiler, type system, and runtime work unlocks a much stronger foundation.

This book examines core concepts such as dispatch, generics, compiler behavior, memory management, and unsafe operations. It also explores metaprogramming and the architectural dynamics that shape large Swift codebases.

By the end of this journey, you will see Swift not just as a tool for writing code, but as a system with clear principles and trade-offs that influence performance, architecture, and scalability.

How to Read This Book

This book is structured to build your understanding of Swift step by step, so reading the chapters in order will give you the best experience. However, if you're already familiar with certain topics, you can jump directly to chapters that focus on compiler internals, unsafe Swift, or architecture.

What's in Store

This book consists of three sections. Each section has a short introduction that describes its chapters, their topics and the overarching themes of the section. Here's a brief overview of the book's sections:

This book is split into 3 main sections:

Section I: Swift Fundamentals & Type System

This section builds a deep understanding of how Swift's type system works and why it behaves the way it does. You'll learn how protocols are dispatched under different contexts, how generics affect performance and specialization, and how existentials and opaque types differ in real-world usage.

The chapters explain method dispatch, static vs dynamic behavior, and the trade-offs between flexibility and compile-time guarantees. By the end, you'll be able to predict how Swift code is compiled and executed simply by looking at its type structure.

Section II: Execution, Concurrency, & The Compiler

The chapters in this section focuses on what happens after code is written but before it runs. You'll follow Swift code through the compiler pipeline, including SIL generation, optimization passes, and machine code emission. It explains ARC, memory layout, and ownership rules, then shows when and how to safely step outside them using Unsafe Swift.

You'll also learn how to use compiler diagnostics and tools to identify performance bottlenecks and write code that is both fast and correct.

Section III: Scalable Architecture & Tooling

This section teaches how to apply these low-level concepts at the system level. You'll learn metaprogramming techniques like reflection, result builders, and macros to reduce boilerplate and enforce consistency.

You'll also learn about modularization, static vs dynamic linking, Swift Package Manager internals, and dependency graphs. The focus is on structuring large codebases for faster builds, clear boundaries, predictable dependencies, and long-term maintainability.

Section I: Swift Fundamentals & Type System

This section builds a deep understanding of how Swift's type system works and why it behaves the way it does. You'll learn how protocols are dispatched under different contexts, how generics affect performance and specialization, and how existentials and opaque types differ in real-world usage.

The chapters explain method dispatch, static vs dynamic behavior, and the trade-offs between flexibility and compile-time guarantees. By the end, you'll be able to predict how Swift code is compiled and executed simply by looking at its type structure.

Chapter 1: Where the Memory Lies

Aaqib Hussain

When writing code, programmers frequently take for granted how smoothly Swift handles memory for us. Unlike earlier languages such as C or Objective-C, which required you to specify object sizes and manually release memory, Swift manages this behind the scenes. Under the hood, Swift makes carefully calculated measures to optimize memory usage. The purpose of this chapter is to guide you through that journey.

This chapter will explore the world of memory management. You'll learn how Swift uses structs to optimize runtime, and when (and when not) they are the right tool for the job. Similarly, how is a class laid out in memory? How does the magic occur? You'll examine how Swift's memory model handles allocation on the stack vs the heap, and how Automatic Reference Counting (ARC) works in practice.

You'll also understand the concepts of Copy-on-Write (CoW) and Value Semantics, and see how they make Swift highly performant and efficient by default. Along the way, you'll build a clearer understanding of ARC and learn how to reason about memory management to avoid common pitfalls.

If you've ever been curious about what occurs when you write something as simple as `let name = "Steve Wozniak"` — this chapter is for you.

Memory Layout Basics: Value vs Reference Types

In Swift, by default, Classes, Actors, and escaping closures are reference types; on the other hand, Structs, Enums, functions, and non-escaping closures are value types. Being conscious of the choice of value and reference types is important to writing performant code.

Fundamentally, Swift allocates memory in two ways: via the stack and the heap. Swift automatically determines whether to use the stack or the heap based on the type of data structure.

- The stack is allocated at runtime in a predictable manner.
- The compiler knows the size and layout of value types, so it can prepare the stack frame size ahead of time.
- The heap is allocated dynamically at runtime.
- For the heap, the compiler doesn't know the exact lifetime or size of reference types in advance, so memory is managed at runtime using Automatic Reference Counting (ARC).

Value types are generally faster in terms of performance and code integrity since they are stored on the stack, which operates on a push-pop mechanism in memory. Imagine the stack like a pile of plates: you can only add a new plate on top or remove the top one. This Last-In, First-Out (LIFO) system is very fast because it's controlled by a simple **stack pointer**. Each time a function runs, a new frame with its local variables is pushed onto the stack. When the function finishes, that frame is popped off. The cost is no more than assigning an integer.

In contrast, reference type objects are stored on the heap, and the pointers to those objects typically reside on the stack or in another heap-allocated structure. Heap allocations are dynamic and complex compared to stack allocations, requiring a more sophisticated memory manager. To allocate memory, Swift searches for an unused block of memory; once it's no longer needed, that memory is returned to the pool. Moreover, because multiple threads may allocate memory simultaneously, the heap must maintain integrity through locking or synchronization mechanisms.

Struct Allocation

Here, let's look at some code and see what Swift is doing behind the scenes:

```
struct Size {
  var width, height: Double
  func area() -> Double {
    return width * height
  }
}

let size1 = Size(width: 0, height: 0) // 1
let size2 = size1 // 2
size2.width = 7 // 3
// use size1
// use size2
print("size1 width: \(size1.width)") // Prints "size1 width:
0.0" // 4
print("size2 width: \(size2.width)") // Prints "size2 width:
7.0" // 5
```

Here is a struct called `Size` that contains two properties: **width** and **height**, along with a method that computes the area.

1. Create an instance, **size1**, with (0, 0) as initial values.
2. Assign **size1** to **size2**.
3. Change the **width** of **size2** to 7.
4. The object of **size1** remains unchanged. Thus, it prints "size1 width: 0.0".
5. Prints "size2 width: 7.0".

Because `Size` is a struct, Swift performs a copy of the instance when executing line `// 2`. At compile time, Swift determines the stack frame and allocates memory on the stack at runtime. The stack pointer is then adjusted to reserve space for the new value.

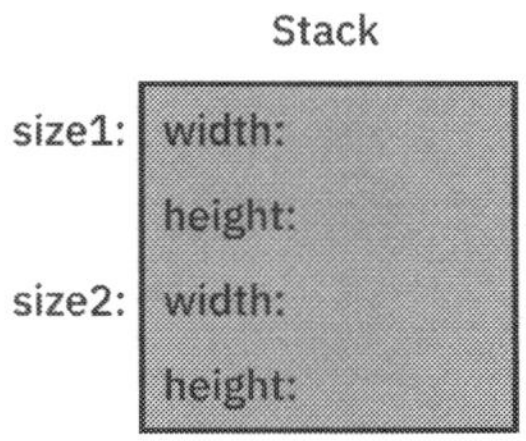

Stack allocated space for width and height

When the code executes (lines 1 and 2), the stack is populated with values for both **size1** and **size2**. A distinct copy of the **size2** instance is made because structs in Swift use value semantics.

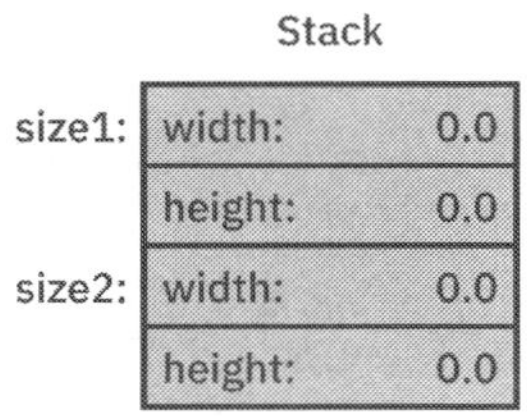

Stack initialized space for width and height

As soon as line 3 executes, the **width** of **size2** is updated to 7. This change does not affect **size1**. This behavior, where changes to one instance do not affect the other, is known as **value semantics**.

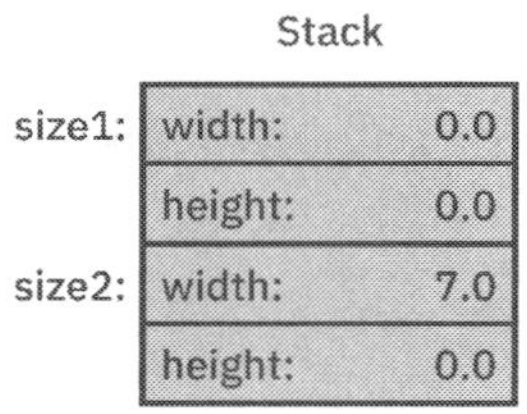

Value changed to 7.0 for width

Swift automatically reclaims memory by moving the stack pointer back when the function or scope in which it was declared exits. This effectively pops the stack, deallocating any local variables or value types stored there.

Class Allocation

In contrast, consider a similar piece of code with a `class`:

```
class Size {
  var width, height: Double
  init(width: Double, height: Double) {
    self.width = width
    self.height = height
  }

  func area() -> Double {
    return width * height
  }
}
```

```
let size1 = Size(width: 0, height: 0) // 1
let size2 = size1 // 2
size2.width = 7 // 3
// use size1
// use size2
```

Here, the memory layout differs from the struct example because `Size` is a reference type. During compilation, Swift infers that `size1` is a reference type. Consequently, at runtime, the stack doesn't store the property values directly; instead, it reserves space only for a memory pointer that points to the instance's location on the heap. The properties themselves live on the heap, rather than being stored inline on the stack.

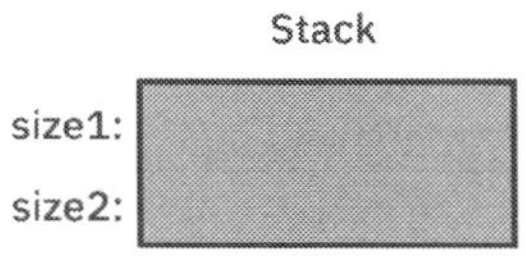

Stack allocated memory for pointers

On the line `//1`, when the variable is initialized, Swift allocates a block of memory on the heap that is larger than the 2 words needed for the properties alone. At a minimum, an additional 2 words are used for runtime metadata.

> **Note**: On a 64-bit macOS system, 1 word = 8 bytes.

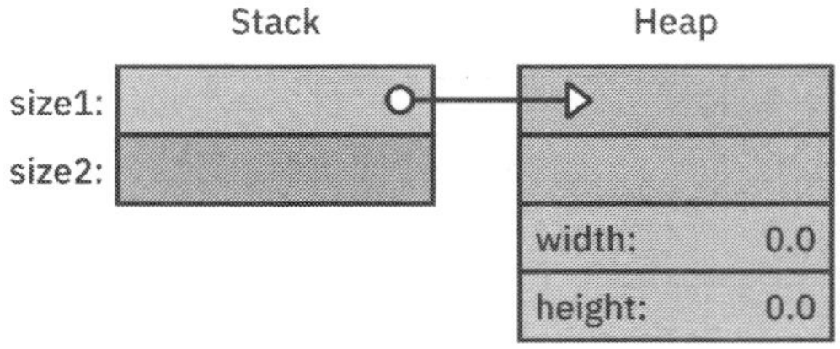

Heap initialized.

The additional two words in a class instance are used to store runtime metadata:

1. The first word typically contains the `isa` pointer, which points to metadata that includes:

- The class type
- Layout and size information

- Virtual method tables (vtables) or method pointers
- Conformance tables
- Superclass metadata

This metadata resides elsewhere in memory. Swift establishes this at compile time and manages it at runtime.

2. The second word refers to Automatic Reference Counting (ARC), which tracks the number of references to an instance.

Now, the code on line `// 2` executes, it assigns the **size1** instance to **size2**. Unlike with a struct, a new copy of the object is not created. Instead, the **size2** reference now points to the same object in the heap as **size1**.

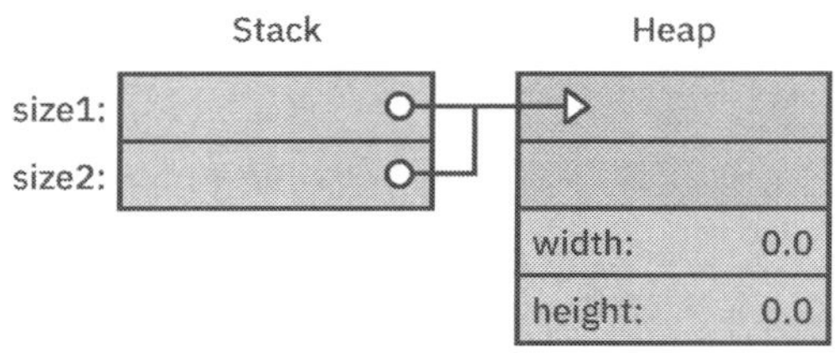

size2 pointing to the same instance on heap.

When the value 7 is assigned to the `width` property of **size2** on line `// 3`, it also updates the `width` property of `size1`. This behavior, known as **reference semantics**, can lead to unintended state sharing if not handled carefully.

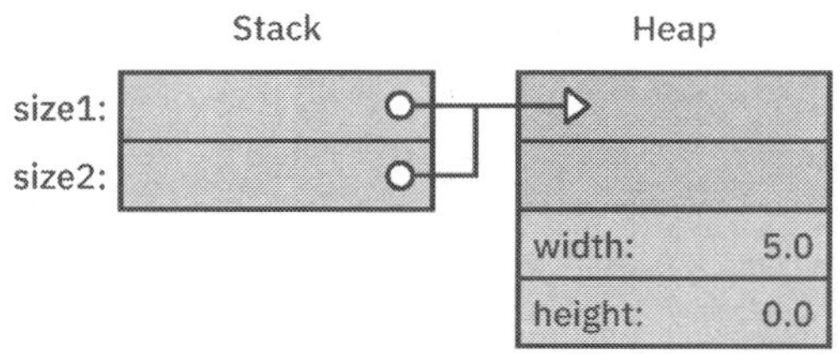

Value change reflects on both instances.

After both instances are no longer in use, ARC will:

- Deallocate the heap memory (if the reference count drops to zero)
- Return it to the heap allocator for reuse, and
- Pop the stack frame if the variable was stored on the stack (such as the reference variables themselves)

Where Allocations Happen

Swift stores the `area()` method in both the struct and class examples in the **code segment**, also known as the **text segment**. This is the read-only part of the app's memory where the compiled machine code instructions are stored.

The main difference is how the method interacts with instance data.

For structs, Swift passes the value directly, and accessing properties like **width** and **height** is efficient without pointer indirection. For classes, Swift implicitly passes a reference to the instance on the heap (`self`). This requires dereferencing the pointer to access properties or call methods, which is slower than stack access and adds the general overhead of managing the object's lifetime via ARC.

Static and class methods are also stored in the code segment, but they do not incur ARC overhead because they neither capture nor depend on instance-level `self`.

Swift stores `static let` variables in the read-only data segment of the binary. These are initialized once at runtime in a thread-safe way and embedded into the binary alongside string literals and global constants.

On the other hand, `static var` is stored in a global data section that supports write operations. Each `static var` has a single shared memory location, and Swift ensures thread-safe initialization.

With `lazy var` or `static lazy var`, the value is only initialized upon first access. Because initialization is deferred, Swift checks at runtime whether the value has already been created; if not, it computes and stores it for future use.

Class within Struct Allocations

Think about an example where a struct contains a class as one of its properties:

```
struct Owner {
  var name: String
  var vehicle: Vehicle
}

class Vehicle {
  var number: String
  init(number: String) {
    self.number = number
  }
}
```

The `Owner` struct is a value type, so it's typically stored on the stack when used in a local scope. However, the `vehicle` property is a reference to a class instance and always lives on the heap.

So what does this mean?

- The `vehicle` inside `Owner` is just a pointer to a `Vehicle` object on the heap.
- Copying an `Owner` value only copies the reference to the `Vehicle`, not the `Vehicle` itself.
- As a result, changes made to `vehicle` through one copy of `Owner` will be reflected in all copies that point to the same `Vehicle` instance.

Struct within Class Allocations

Imagine a case where a class contains a struct as one of its properties:

```
struct Position {
  var x: Int
  var y: Int
}

class Player {
  var name: String
  var position: Position
  init(name: String, position: Position) {
    self.name = name
    self.position = position
  }
}
```

The `Player` class is a reference type, which means its instances are always allocated on the heap. The `position` property, being a struct, is stored inline within the class's heap-allocated memory block - rather than on the stack.

So what does this mean?

- The `Position` is not stored on the stack; it's part of the `Player`'s heap allocation.
- However, since `Position` is a value type, it still exhibits value semantics.
- This means if you assign or mutate `position` in one instance of `Player`, it will not affect another instance, unlike a class reference.

Enum and Actor Allocations

Just like structs, enums are value types, and Swift typically allocates them on the stack. If the enum becomes too large or is captured by an escaping closure, Swift may allocate it on the heap, similarly to large structs. Despite that, enums retain their value semantics, meaning when you assign or pass them, Swift makes a copy.

Similarly, actors are reference types, just as classes are. They are always allocated on the heap, and variables referencing them are stored on the stack. Under the hood, actors behave like classes in terms of memory layout, with the additional layer of isolation for safe concurrency. They also include runtime metadata, ARC reference counters, and method dispatch information, just as classes do.

Other Special Cases of Allocations

Aside from the memory allocation behaviors discussed earlier, there are some cases worth looking into:

1. Structs that are Too Large
2. Structs Captured by Escaping Closures

Structs that are Too Large

If a struct contains a very large amount of data, Swift may choose to allocate it on the heap to avoid overflowing the stack.

```
struct WholeLottaData {
  var data = [Int](repeating: 0, count: 1_000_000)
}
```

In this case:

- The `data` property is a heap-allocated array regardless (since `Array` is a reference type).
- However, if the struct contains multiple large properties or is used in a context where large copies are made, Swift may choose to store the entire struct on the heap to improve performance and avoid excessive stack usage.

Structs Captured By Escaping Closures

When a struct is captured inside an escaping closure, it may be stored on the heap. This is because the closure may outlive the stack frame where the struct was originally defined.

```
struct SomeTask {
  var id: Int
}

class ViewController {
  var closure: (() -> Void)?

  func schedule() {
    let task = SomeTask(id: 42)

    closure = {
      print("Task ID is \(task.id)")
    }
  }
}
```

Here's what's happening:

- Since the closure escapes the `schedule()` function, any captured variables must outlive the function's stack frame.
- Swift stores the captured **task** struct on the heap to ensure its lifetime extends safely.
- Even if a struct is stored on the heap, it retains its **value semantics**.

Allocation Summary

Here is the summarized overview of what was discussed earlier:

Type	Kind	Default Allocation	Notes
`struct`	Value type	Stack (usually)	Stored inline; can move to the heap if becomes large or is captured by an escaping closure.
`class`	Reference type	Heap	Always heap-allocated; accessed via a reference stored on the stack.
`enum`	Value type	Stack (usually)	Same behavior as `struct`; stored inline unless large or captured.
`actor`	Reference type	Heap	Like `class`, but with built-in concurrency isolation at runtime.

Summary of Memory Allocations

Anatomy of Swift Types in Memory

Swift provides a utility `MemoryLayout<T>`, which offers valuable insights into how a type is laid out in memory. It gives you three key properties:

`size`: the number of bytes used to store the instance (excluding any padding added due to alignment),`stride`: the number of bytes from the start of one instance to the start of the next in contiguous memory (includes padding),`alignment`: the required byte alignment for the type in memory.

This section analyzes how different Swift types, **structs**, **classes**, **enums**, and **actors** are represented in memory, how memory alignment and padding affect layout, and what hidden costs may be involved.

Struct Memory Layout

Structs are typically stored inline on the stack, so their memory layout is usually tightly packed. However, Swift may add padding to properly align the data. Consider the following `struct`:

```
struct Point {
  let x: Double // 8 bytes
  let y: Double // 8 bytes
  let isFilled: Bool // 1 byte
}
```

You can inspect the memory layout using:

```
print(MemoryLayout<Point>.size) // 17
print(MemoryLayout<Point>.stride) // 24
print(MemoryLayout<Point>.alignment) // 8
```

Take a look at the diagram below; it illustrates how Swift lays out this struct in memory:

1. **Size** is 17 bytes (8 + 8 + 1).
2. **Stride** is 24 bytes. Swift pads the remaining unused space to meet the alignment requirements.
3. **Alignment** is 8 bytes. `Double` in Swift takes up 8 bytes and is the largest in this struct.

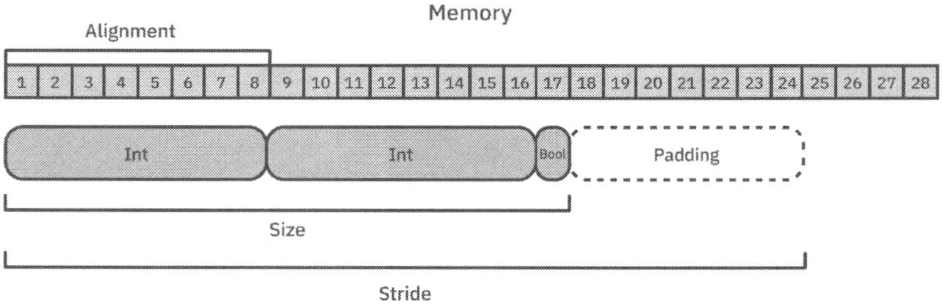

Hypothetical Swift struct memory layout demonstrating alignment, padding, size, and stride.

Due to alignment rules, even though only 17 bytes are needed, Swift pads the `Point` to 24 bytes to ensure proper alignment in memory. This way, any subsequent value stored after this `struct` will start at byte 25, ensuring proper alignment and efficient memory access.

Class Memory Layout

In the case of classes, unlike structs, the actual values are not stored inline on the stack. Instead, a reference (or pointer) to the instance is stored on the stack, while the actual object is allocated on the heap.

Look at the following code:

```
class Vehicle {
  var speed: Int
  var isRunning: Bool
  init(speed: Int, isRunning: Bool) {
    self.speed = speed
    self.isRunning = isRunning
  }
}
```

If you inspect its layout using `MemoryLayout`:

```
print(MemoryLayout<Vehicle>.size) // Size of the reference value
(usually 8 bytes)
print(MemoryLayout<Vehicle>.stride)
print(MemoryLayout<Vehicle>.alignment)
```

This will return the size of the reference, which is usually 8 bytes on 64-bit systems, not the size of the actual object in memory.

To inspect the size of the actual class instance stored on the heap, you can use the code below:

```
print(class_getInstanceSize(Vehicle.self)) // 32 bytes
```

Heap	
0x08	16 bytes isa pointer + class metadata
0x09	8 speed (Int)
0x10	1 isRunning (Bool)
0x11	7 Padding
Total size: 32 bytes	

Hypothetical class memory layout demonstrating metadata and paddings.

Here's how it works:

1. 16 bytes are reserved for internal use by the runtime, typically including the `isa` pointer and other metadata such as reference counts and alignment buffers.
2. The class has an `Int` and a `Bool`, consisting of 8 bytes and 1 byte, respectively.
3. Swift pads the instance to align to the largest member (`Int`, 8 bytes), adding 7 bytes of padding after the `Bool`.

Enum Memory Layout

Enums in Swift are stored similarly to structs, but with one key difference: they need an extra byte (or more) to track which case is currently active. This is often referred to as the **discriminator** or **tag**.

Check the code example below:

```
enum Result {
  case success(Int)
  case failure(String)
}
```

To examine the memory layout, run the code below:

```
print(MemoryLayout<Result>.size) // 17
print(MemoryLayout<Result>.stride) // 24
print(MemoryLayout<Result>.alignment) // 8
```

Here's a deconstruction of each line:

1. Size is 8 + 8 + 1, a total of 17 bytes, with 8 for the associated value of `Int`, 8 for the `String`, and 1 for storing the tag.
2. Stride is 24 bytes.
3. Alignment is 8 bytes because the largest member requires 8-byte alignment.

Actor Memory Layout

Actors are reference types in Swift. Like classes, they are stored on the heap, with a reference to the instance held on the stack.

However, the Swift runtime may allocate additional memory to support concurrency guarantees, including internal queues, isolation state, or locking mechanisms to ensure thread safety.

```
actor Counter {
  var value = 0
}
```

To check the layout for an `actor`, do as follows:

```
print(class_getInstanceSize(Counter.self)) // 120
```

The `120` bytes reported include:

1. 16 bytes for internal metadata (e.g., `isa` pointer and reference count).
2. 8 bytes for the `Int` property.
3. 96 bytes reserved for the actor's runtime internals related to isolation and scheduling.

Thus, even a minimal actor has a larger memory footprint than a class due to its built-in concurrency support.

ARC: Automatic Reference Counting

ARC (Automatic Reference Counting) is Swift's memory management system for reference types, such as classes and actors. Every time a new reference to an instance is created, ARC increments a reference count stored alongside the instance in the heap. This count helps the Swift runtime determine that the object is still in use and should not be deallocated.

As references are removed, the count is decremented. Once it drops to zero, Swift deallocates the instance and reclaims the memory.

When a new strong reference to an instance is created, ARC increases its reference count (an operation called a **retain**). When a reference is destroyed, such as when a variable goes out of scope, the count decreases (a **release**). Once the count reaches zero, Swift deallocates the instance. To support multi-threaded access, these retain and release operations are often performed using atomic operations, especially in the presence of concurrency. This ensures that even when multiple threads access or release references simultaneously, the reference count remains accurate. While this safety is necessary, it does introduce a small performance overhead.

> **Note**: An atomic operation is one that cannot be interrupted by other threads, is not prone to race conditions, and completes as a single, indivisible step.

ARC Pitfalls: Retain Cycle

While ARC is powerful, it can cause a specific issue called a strong reference cycle (or **retain cycle**). This occurs when two or more objects hold strong references to each other, forming a loop that prevents them from being deallocated. This is a common type of memory leak.

To fix this, Swift provides two keywords: `weak` and `unowned`. You only need these tools to break retain cycles; they are not intended for everyday use.

`weak` tells the Swift runtime that this particular reference should not increment the instance's reference count. The referenced instance can become `nil` at any point, so the reference must be declared optional.

`unowned` also does not increase the reference count, but assumes the referenced instance will always be available during the lifetime of the reference. It must be non-optional, and if the instance gets deallocated and the reference is accessed, it will crash at runtime.

Take a look at how weak works:

```
class Person {
  var name: String
  var pet: Pet?
  init(name: String) {
    self.name = name
  }
```

```
  deinit {
    print("\(name) is being deallocated")
  }
}

class Pet {
  var name: String
  weak var owner: Person? // weak reference to avoid retain
cycle

  init(name: String) {
    self.name = name
  }

  deinit {
    print("\(name) is being deallocated")
  }
}

// ...

var john: Person? = Person(name: "John")
var dog: Pet? = Pet(name: "Buddy")
john?.pet = dog
dog?.owner = john
john = nil
dog = nil
```

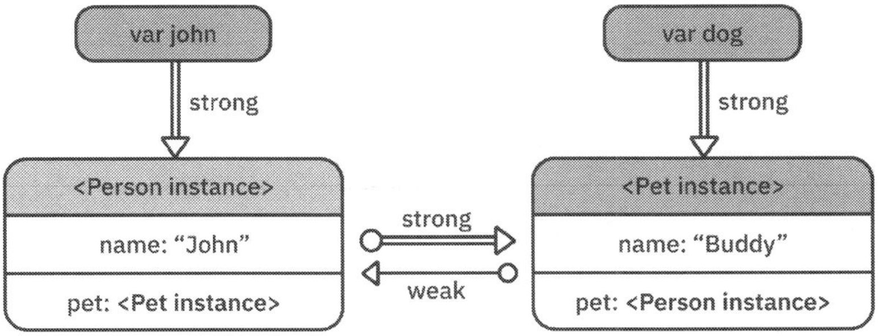

Breaking a strong reference with weak.

If `owner` had been a strong reference, setting `john = nil` would not have deallocated the `Person` instance because `dog` would still hold a strong reference to it, resulting in a retain cycle.

This scenario is illustrated below:

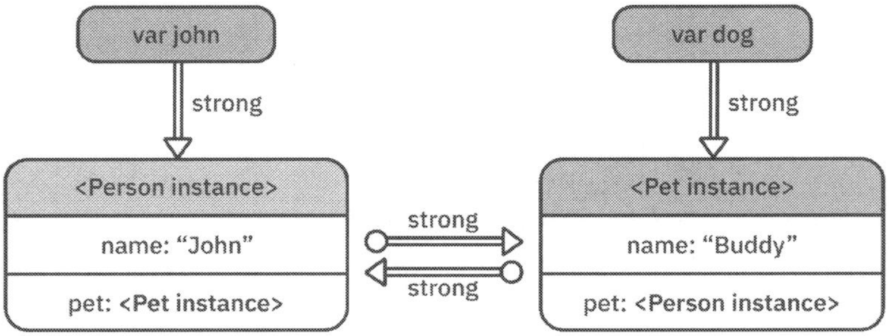

Retain cycle exists due to strong references.

Similarly, check the example of unowned:

```
class Customer {
  let name: String
  var card: CreditCard?
  init(name: String) {
    self.name = name
  }
  deinit {
    print("\(name) is being deallocated")
  }
}


class CreditCard {
  let number: UInt64
  unowned let customer: Customer // unowned because customer
always owns the card
  init(number: UInt64, customer: Customer) {
    self.number = number
    self.customer = customer
  }
  deinit {
    print("Card #\(number) is being deallocated")
  }
}

// ...

var alice: Customer? = Customer(name: "Alice")
alice?.card = CreditCard(number: 1234_5678_9012_3456, customer:
alice!)
alice = nil
```

Here, `CreditCard` holds an `unowned` reference to `Customer`. Since the card cannot exist without the customer, this avoids a retain cycle.

Retain Cycles in Closures

Closures can also capture `self` strongly, causing retain cycles, especially with escaping closures. This is common when a class instance holds a closure property or passes a closure to something that stores it beyond the current scope.

In older versions of Swift, `self` was captured implicitly, which could easily lead to accidental retain cycles. Modern Swift helps by requiring you to explicitly write `self.` inside a closure, making the capture clear. However, this doesn't prevent retain cycles; it only makes you aware of the capture.

Check the following example:

```
class ViewModel {
  var name = "Steve"
  var onUpdate: (() -> Void)?
  func setup() {
    onUpdate = {
      print(self.name) // self is captured strongly here
    }
  }
  deinit {
    print("ViewModel deinitialized")
  }
}

// ...

var vm: ViewModel? = ViewModel()
vm?.setup()
vm = nil // deinit won't be called due to retain cycle
```

To fix this issue, `self` can be made `[weak self]` or `[unowned self]` to break the retain cycle.

```
func setup() {
  onUpdate = { [weak self] in
    print(self?.name ?? "nil")
  }
}
```

When to use which:

1. Use weak when self can become `nil`, and you want to avoid crashes.

2. Use unowned when you're sure `self` will still be alive when the closure runs; otherwise, it will crash at runtime.

What does not create a retain cycle?

```
class ViewModel {
  var onUpdate: (() -> Void)?
  func setup() {
    let name = "Steve"
    onUpdate = {
      print(name)
    }
  }
  deinit {
    print("ViewModel deinitialized")
  }
}

// ...

var viewModel: ViewModel? = ViewModel()
viewModel?.setup()
viewModel = nil // deinit gets called due to no retain cycle
```

Since `self` is not captured in this closure, there's no retain cycle, and the object is deallocated as expected.

Retain Cycles in Delegates

Retain cycles often occur in delegation patterns if the delegate is strongly referenced. Consider the following example:

```
protocol DownloaderDelegate: AnyObject {
  func downloadDidFinish()
}

class Downloader {
  var delegate: DownloaderDelegate?  //  This is a strong
reference!

  deinit {
    print("Downloader deinitialized")
  }

  func startDownload() {
    // simulate some work
    delegate?.downloadDidFinish()
  }
}

class ViewController: DownloaderDelegate {
  var downloader: Downloader?
```

```
  init() {
    downloader = Downloader()
    downloader?.delegate = self  // self strongly owns
downloader, and downloader strongly owns self
  }

  func downloadDidFinish() {
    print("Download finished")
  }

  deinit {
    print("ViewController deinitialized")
  }
}

// ...

var viewController: ViewController? = ViewController()
viewController = nil  // Neither deinit is called due to retain
cycle
```

Here, a retain cycle exists because `ViewController` strongly owns the `Downloader`, and the `Downloader` strongly owns its delegate, which is `ViewController`.

To fix it, you can declare the delegate as weak:

```
weak var delegate: DownloaderDelegate?
```

Now, re-running:

```
var viewController: ViewController? = ViewController()
viewController = nil  // Both deinit methods are called – no
retain cycle
```

The retain cycle is eliminated because `Downloader` no longer retains its delegate strongly. `delegate` is a weak reference, so it doesn't increase the reference count of `ViewController`. Thus, when `viewController` is set to `nil`, both objects are properly deallocated.

Copy-on-Write

Copy-on-write is a performance optimization Swift applies to certain value types, such as `Array`, `Set`, `Dictionary`, `Data`, and `String`.
When you assign these value types to a new variable, Swift doesn't immediately create a new copy of the underlying data; both variables point to the same instance in memory.

Only when one of the variables attempts to mutate the data does Swift create a copy to keep the original value.

Take a look at the following example:

```
var array1 = [1, 2, 3]
var array2 = array1 // No copy yet — same underlying buffer
array2.append(4)     // Now a copy happens
```

Even though these value types are structs, they store their underlying data (like buffers, character storage, or hash tables) in the heap. Swift leverages the **Copy-on-Write** mechanism to ensure optimization.

Before making a mutation, Swift checks if the buffer is uniquely owned and that no other references point to it. If it is, the mutation is applied directly to the existing buffer.

On the other hand, if the buffer is shared, Swift creates a real copy and then applies the mutation to the new buffer to preserve value semantics.

This uniqueness check is typically performed using a function such as `isKnownUniquelyReferenced`, which determines whether a reference to a class instance is unique or shared.

Consider the following class:

```
final class Buffer {
  var storage: [Int]
  init(_ storage: [Int]) {
    self.storage = storage
  }
}

// ...

var buffer1 = Buffer([1, 2, 3])
var buffer2 = buffer1

print(isKnownUniquelyReferenced(&buffer1)) // false — shared
with buffer2

buffer2 = Buffer(buffer2.storage) // simulate CoW — now buffer1
is unique

print(isKnownUniquelyReferenced(&buffer1)) // true — no longer
shared
```

This example demonstrates Copy-on-Write behavior: initially, `buffer1` is shared with `buffer2`, but after `buffer2` is reassigned to a new instance, `buffer1` becomes uniquely referenced.

Optimizing Swift Memory Behavior

While writing code, you shouldn't just think of it as getting the job done, but think of it like developing the foundation of a ship. If the foundation is strong, it's going to sail through rough times with ease. But if the foundation is weak, the ship will start leaking and become unbalanced.

Your code is no different. If you don't think it through before writing, especially when it comes to memory management, it may lead to leaks, performance issues, and long-term headaches.

When to Use Value vs Reference Types

Choosing between a value or reference type depends on several factors. If you're aiming for predictability and isolation, go with a value type. When identity and shared mutable state matter, a reference type is usually the better option.

Value types provide safer, simpler memory behavior, especially with optimizations like Copy-on-Write, but copying large data structures frequently can be expensive. On the other hand, reference types allow shared memory access but bring along the overhead of ARC.

Consider this practical example to help you understand these trade-offs and write better and more efficient code.

Example: Caching Avatars

Look at the following code sample:

```
enum AvatarStyle { case cartoon, realistic, pixel }
enum Mood { case happy, serious, surprised }
enum Accessory { case none, glasses, hat }


var avatarCache = [String: UIImage]() // 1

func generateAvatar(style: AvatarStyle, mood: Mood, accessory:
Accessory) -> UIImage {
  let cacheKey = "\(style)-\(mood)-\(accessory)" // 2

  if let cachedAvatar = avatarCache[cacheKey] {
    return cachedAvatar
```

```
    }

    // Placeholder avatar generation
    let avatar = UIImage() // Pretend this is generated with the
given options

    avatarCache[cacheKey] = avatar
    return avatar
}
```

Consider that you're developing an app that displays a list of users who have signed up on your app. Behind the list is a method that creates an avatar based on the `Style`, `Mood`, and `Accessory` you pass as arguments. To avoid recreating the same avatar, a dictionary is used to check whether a similar avatar exists based on the passed enums. The method creates a key based on serializing the passed enums.

Now here is the problem, this method is called every time a scroll event occurs in a `TableViewController`. If you recall, even though `String` is a value type, its contents are often stored on the heap, especially when the string gets longer or is dynamically constructed. So, every time this method runs during a scroll, Swift allocates and hashes a new key, which adds avoidable overhead.

Using a `String` key is also less type-safe. If you ever refactor your enums or misspell a string interpolation, it could silently break the caching logic. A struct enforces type correctness at compile time.

Define a new struct like this:

```
struct AvatarConfiguration: Hashable {
    var style: AvatarStyle
    var mood: Mood
    var accessory: Accessory
}
```

Update your cache and key as follows:

```
var avatarCache = [AvatarConfiguration: UIImage]()
let cacheKey = AvatarConfiguration(style: style, mood: mood,
accessory: accessory)
```

Why does it work?

Because structs are first-class types in Swift. For this reason, structs can be used as dictionary keys. And since `AvatarConfiguration` is a struct, it's a value type that avoids heap indirection and gives better performance for this use case.

Pretty cool, huh?

Note: Heap indirection, in this context, refers to following a pointer to access the actual data that lives on the heap. With a struct, the data lives inline on the stack, avoiding the extra lookup, which can improve performance.

Example: Safer Document Struct

Take a look at the following code:

```
struct Document {
  let path: URL
  let identifier: String
  let fileType: String
  init(path: URL, identifier: String, fileType: String) {
    self.path = path
    self.identifier = identifier
    self.fileType = fileType
  }
}
```

Furthermore, consider that the app you're working on also supports users' document uploads. The document has:

1. A `path` of type `URL`
2. An `identifier` of type `String`
3. A `fileType` of type `String`

At first glance, this struct looks fine. But take a closer look. This struct includes types like `String` and `URL`, which often store their contents on the heap, leading to more allocation overhead, especially when used frequently.

There is also a type-safety concern. In the `identifier` variable, you can pass a **"abc"** or **"123"**. Similarly, in `fileType`, you can pass **"doc"**, **"john"**, or **"xyz"**. This may not only cause performance issues but also underlying bugs that would be harder to catch in more complex systems.

Something should be done about it.

First, replace the `identifier: String` with `identifier: UUID`. Swift's **Foundation** framework provides a 128-bit randomly generated identifier, which is ideal here. It's more type-safe, more compact, and, in many cases, more stack-friendly.

Then, the next step is to fix the file type issue.

```
enum DocType: String {
  case pdf
  case docx
  case pages
}
```

Using an enum here avoids raw string literals scattered in your codebase. It's easier to refactor, harder to misuse, and you can still get the raw value if needed.So, your improved struct becomes:

```
struct Document {
  let path: URL
  let identifier: UUID
  let fileType: DocType
  init(path: URL, identifier: UUID, fileType: DocType) {
    self.path = path
    self.identifier = identifier
    self.fileType = fileType
  }
}
```

Although these may seem like small changes, they add up. Thinking about memory behavior, type safety, and allocation costs helps you write code that's not only efficient but also easier to reason about, maintain, and refactor in the long run.

You should always aim to build ships sturdy enough to withstand any storm.

Minimizing ARC Overhead

As discussed earlier, reference types come with ARC overhead, and you even walked through some examples. As a programmer, your goal should be to write code that minimizes this overhead wherever possible.

Here are a few tips to keep your code in check:

Not Everything Has to Be a Class

Avoid using classes unless identity or shared mutable state is truly needed. If not, prefer structs or enums. Value types are generally safer and more efficient in terms of memory.

Break Strong References

Strong reference cycles are sneaky. Closures and delegates are the usual suspects. Use `weak` or `unowned` references where appropriate to prevent retain cycles.

Keep Classes Small

The larger and more tightly coupled your classes are, the harder ARC has to work. Smaller, focused classes not only reduce ARC overhead but also make your code easier to reason about and test.

Measuring and Debugging Memory

Understanding memory and how it works is one thing, but measuring it as it plays out is another. Without seeing how your app behaves in real-world scenarios, you can only infer behavior.

Thankfully, Apple provides powerful tools to measure those insights — monitoring allocations, catching leaks, and spotting inefficiencies early on.

Instruments (Allocations and Leaks)

Xcode provides a profiling tool to check for allocations and memory leaks. It's an essential tool for diagnosing memory-related issues. Whether you want to trace memory allocations or detect leaks, it's your go-to.

Memory Graph Debugger

Xcode's built-in tool gives you a visual representation of retain cycles. It shows how many active instances of a class are in memory and how they're being retained. You can see the entire graph of object relationships at a glance.

> **Tip**: Make it a habit to check these insights during development, not later. It's always easier to catch and fix things early than to untangle memory messes at the end.

Key Points

- Swift manages memory for you under the hood, but understanding how it works helps you write more efficient, faster, safer, and more predictable code.
- Structs and Enums are value types. Classes and Actors are reference types.
- Value types are stored on the stack, and reference types are stored on the heap and managed using ARC.
- Structs and Enums use value semantics, meaning they are copied rather than shared. Classes and Actors rely on reference semantics, meaning they refer to the same shared instance.
- Swift optimizes value types using **Copy-on-Write (CoW)**. Even though value types are copied, the copy only happens when a change is made. CoW in `Array`, `Dictionary`, `Set`, `Data`, and `String` helps avoid unnecessary memory duplication.
- Structs are stored inline in memory, but if they become too large, they may be heap-allocated.
- Classes include hidden metadata such as the `isa` pointer and reference counter, which increases the overall memory cost.
- Actors are like classes but come with built-in concurrency and isolation, resulting in a larger memory footprint.
- ARC keeps track of references to class and actor instances. Once the count drops to zero, the memory is deallocated.
- ARC operations are often atomic to ensure thread safety, but they come with some performance overhead.
- Retain cycles can sneak into objects through strong references, especially in closures and delegates, which are often the most common culprits of memory leaks.
- Choose a value type when you're aiming for predictability and isolation. Use a reference type when identity and shared state matter.
- Tools like **Instruments (Allocations & Leaks)** and the **Memory Graph Debugger** in Xcode help you track memory usage and visually detect leaks.
- Build sturdy ships: keep classes small, break strong references, and reach for value types first when they fit the scenario.

Where to Go From Here?

Now that you've peeked under the hood of how Swift's memory management works, you're better equipped to reason about performance, structure your types with clarity, and avoid common ARC pitfalls such as retain cycles and excessive heap allocations.

Up next, you'll look at the different types of dispatch and how protocols further shape your code's behavior at both compile time and runtime.

Chapter 2: Protocols, Dispatch, Existential Types

Aaqib Hussain

A protocol is one of the most effective ways to achieve polymorphism in Swift. Protocols work flawlessly with both classes and structs. Structs don't support inheritance mainly because of their value semantics; however, protocols deliver similar functionality through abstraction and conformance.

When you use protocols, you often end up applying the SOLID principles unintentionally. And that's a good thing. Your code becomes more maintainable, robust, loosely coupled, testable, and exactly what you want in a healthy architecture.

However, protocols aren't all sunshine and rainbows. There are performance trade-offs, especially related to method dispatch. Not all dispatch types are costly; some are lightning-fast.

And what about Generics and Existentials? What's their purpose? How do they differ? When should you choose one over the other? You'll explore all of that in this chapter.

Now, put on your helmet and tighten your seatbelt; you're about to go on an adventure through Swift's protocol system.

Protocol Me This

A protocol is like a *promise*; if you agree to it, you *must fulfill it*. In Swift, you call this *conformance*. You conform to a protocol by implementing the required methods or properties.

Here's a simple example:

```
protocol DataRepository {
  func fetch()
}

struct RemoteDataRepository: DataRepository {
  func fetch() {
    // fetch some data
  }
}
```

The cool thing about protocols? You can provide default implementations.

```
protocol Decoder {
  func decode()
}

extension Decoder {
  func decode() {
    print("Some Default Decoding")
  }
}

struct DefaultDecoder: Decoder {}
```

Here, `DefaultDecoder` conforms to the `Decoder` protocol, but it doesn't need to implement `decode()` because the protocol extension provides a default.So if you do:

```
let defaultDecoder = DefaultDecoder()
defaultDecoder.decode() // Some Default Decoding
```

Default implementations help reduce boilerplate code, like in the example above, and allow you to simulate optional behavior in protocols. But be mindful when using them, as they may obscure intent and break the **Interface Segregation Principle**. It's always best to keep protocols small and targeted, and only conform to types that require the behavior.

Conditional Conformance

Swift also supports conditional conformance, meaning a type only conforms to a protocol under specific conditions. For example:

```
protocol Summable { // 1
  func sum() -> Int
}

extension Array: Summable where Element == Int { // 2
  func sum() -> Int {
    return self.reduce(0, +)
  }
}

let numbers: [Int] = [1, 2, 3, 4, 5] // 3

let total = numbers.sum() // 4
```

To understand what is happening here:

1. A protocol `Summable` with a method `sum()`.
2. `Array` conforms to the `Summable` protocol and implements the `sum()` method only when the `Element` of the array is an `Int`.
3. Initialize an array of integers, named **numbers**.
4. The `sum()` method is available for arrays of integers.

This is a powerful way of extending behavior only where it's appropriate, keeping your code expressive and type-safe.

Dispatch

Now the *million-dollar question*: how does Swift decide which implementation to call? That's what **dispatch** is all about. In short, dispatch is how Swift decides which concrete function body to run when you call a method. Swift uses three primary dispatch mechanisms:

- Static Dispatch
- Dynamic Dispatch
- V-Table (Virtual Table) Dispatch

- Protocol Witness Table
- Message Dispatch

Each dispatch type comes with its performance trade-offs. Understanding when Swift uses which can help you write code that's fast, efficient, and predictable.

Static Dispatch

It's one of the fastest method call mechanisms Swift offers. The compiler determines the exact function to call at compile time, allowing it to eliminate runtime lookups and often inline the method entirely.

It's like saying:

> **I'm fast. I'm very fast.**

It comes into play when you invoke a method from within:

1. A value type, i.e, `struct` or `enum`.
2. A `final` class or a `final` method.

Since Swift knows everything at compile time, it can optimize everything **inline**. It eliminates **indirection**, resulting in faster machine code.

> **Inline**: A compiler optimization that replaces a method call with the method's body to reduce call overhead and enable additional optimizations.

> **Indirection**: Occurs when your code passes through an intermediate layer, such as a reference, container, or dispatch table, before reaching the actual implementation.

```
struct Size {
  var width, height: Double
  func area() -> Double {
    return width * height
  }
}
```

```
let size = Size(width: 10, height: 10)
size.area() // Static Dispatch
```

Similarly, with classes:

```
final class Size {
  var width, height: Double
  func area() -> Double {
    return width * height
  }
}

// OR

class Size {
  var width, height: Double
  final func area() -> Double {
    return width * height
  }
}

let size = Size(width: 10, height: 10)
size.area() // Static Dispatch
```

For protocols:

```
protocol Animal {}

extension Animal {
  func sleep() {
    print("Sleeping soundly.")
  }
}

struct Dog: Animal {}

// OR

class Dog: Animal {}

let animal: Animal = Dog()
animal.sleep() // "Sleeping soundly."
```

A `protocol` with a default implementation for a method that isn't declared in the requirement list uses **static dispatch**, because conforming types aren't required to implement it — regardless of whether it's a `class`, `struct`, or `actor`.

By design, `fileprivate`, `private`, and `static` methods also follow static dispatch. Swift knows at compile time that these methods cannot be overridden, so there's no need for another dispatch mechanism.

Dynamic Dispatch

A call resolution technique in which the exact implementation is determined at runtime via indirection.

Here's a simple analogy to give you a better understanding:

> **Sometimes I'll start a method call, and I don't even know where it's going. I just hope I find it along the way - like an improv conversation. An improversation.**

Swift uses dynamic dispatch when the compiler isn't sure at compile time which method to invoke. Depending on the context, one of the following approaches steps in:

- **V-Table dispatch** for a class inheritance or when a subclass overrides a method from the superclass.
- **Protocol Witness tables** for protocols to find the correct implementation to invoke.
- **Message dispatch** for interoperability with Objective-C.

Virtual Table Dispatch

Virtual dispatch occurs for all members of a class or actor unless specified otherwise.

Each class has a v-table, a list of method pointers. When a method is overridden in a subclass, that subclass updates its v-table entry for that method to point to the new implementation. When a method is called, Swift checks the instance's runtime type, looks up the correct entry in the v-table, and then calls it.

```
class Animal {
  func sleep() {
    print("Sleeping...")
  }
}

class Dog: Animal {
  override func sleep() {
    print("Dog is sleeping.")
  }
}
```

```
let animal: Animal = Dog()
animal.sleep() // V-Table Dispatch
```

At compile time, Swift knows that `sleep()` might be overridden, so it avoids static dispatch. Instead, it generates code that performs a v-table lookup at runtime to determine which method to call.

This adds a bit of indirection but enables dynamic behavior like overriding, which is crucial for polymorphism.

Protocol Witness Table

Whenever you use a protocol with required methods and call them through a protocol type variable, Swift performs a Protocol Witness Table dispatch. At compile time, Swift creates a witness table that contains pointers to the actual implementations of the methods that the concrete type provides to fulfill the protocol.

```
protocol Animal {
  func sleep()
}

class Dog: Animal {
  func sleep() {
    print("Dog is sleeping.")
  }
}

let animal: Animal = Dog()
animal.sleep() // PW-Table Dispatch
```

When you assign a value to a protocol-typed variable, Swift creates an **existential container**. This container holds the value, a pointer to the concrete type's metadata, and a pointer to the protocol witness table.

If you were to do:

```
let animal: Dog = Dog()
animal.sleep() // V-Table Dispatch
```

It reverts to using v-table dispatch because you're no longer using the protocol-typed variable.

It resembles v-table dispatch, but it's not the same. The main difference is that it includes one extra step. In the case of v-table dispatch, the existential container isn't present. This results in slightly higher overhead than v-table dispatch.

Message Dispatch

You often use it daily when working with Swift, but it may never have crossed your mind. Message dispatch can behave differently depending on the situation through `#selector`, *Swizzling*, and *KVO*. Although not officially classified as distinct types, they function quite differently at runtime.

Take a look at the example below:

```
class ViewController: UIViewController {
  override func viewDidLoad() {
    super.viewDidLoad()

    let button = UIButton()
    //...
    button.addTarget(self, action: #selector(buttonAction), for:
.touchUpInside)
  }

  @objc func buttonAction() {
    // some action
  }
}
```

A `#selector` sends the method's name as a message to the button object. The Objective-C runtime uses this method name to find the correct implementation in the object's class and executes it. The `@objc` keyword ensures that the method is visible to the Objective-C runtime.

> **Objective-C Runtime**:
>
> It's a framework that provides the core functionality for Objective-C. It's linked to your Swift app whenever you use things like `@objc`, `#selector`, or KVO. Internally, it handles critical runtime tasks, including **message dispatch**, **method swizzling**, and **dynamic method resolution.**It also plays a key role when building bridge layers between Objective-C and other languages or when you're working with low-level debugging.

When it comes to method swizzling, the Objective-C runtime alters a class's method table by swapping the implementation pointer of the original method with that of the new method, effectively redirecting the dispatch.

```
extension UIViewController {
  @objc func track_viewDidLoad() {
    print("View Did Load: \(String(describing: type(of:
```

```
self)))")
    self.track_viewDidLoad()
  }

  static func swizzleViewDidLoad() {
    let originalSelector = #selector(viewDidLoad)
    let swizzledSelector = #selector(track_viewDidLoad)

    guard let originalMethod = class_getInstanceMethod(self,
originalSelector),
          let swizzledMethod = class_getInstanceMethod(self,
swizzledSelector) else {
      return
    }

    method_exchangeImplementations(originalMethod,
swizzledMethod)
  }
}
```

In **Key-Value-Observing (KVO)**, the Objective-C runtime generates a hidden subclass of the observed object's class. At runtime, the object's class is replaced with this hidden subclass, which overrides the property's setter to add KVO logic.

```
class ViewModelObserver {
  let viewModel: ViewModel
  private var valueObservation: NSKeyValueObservation?

  init(viewModel: ViewModel) {
    self.viewModel = viewModel

    self.valueObservation = viewModel.observe(\.value, options:
[.old, .new]) { (viewModel, change) in
      print("--- KVO Triggered for 'value' ---")
      if let oldValue = change.oldValue, let newValue =
change.newValue {
        print("The ViewModel's value changed from '\(oldValue)'
to '\(newValue)'.")
      }
    }
  }
}

final class ViewModel: NSObject {
  @objc dynamic var value: String // 1

  init(value: String) {
    self.value = value
    super.init()
  }
}
```

The property inside the `ViewModel` is marked with the `dynamic` keyword. This explicitly instructs the Objective-C runtime to use message dispatch. Otherwise, by default, Swift would use v-table dispatch here because it's inside a class.

Message dispatch is considerably slower than v-table and static dispatch, but it is the foundation of many dynamic features inherited from Objective-C.

Flowchart for Dispatch

Here's a simple flowchart to visualize how Swift decides which dispatch mechanism to use based on the context of the method call:

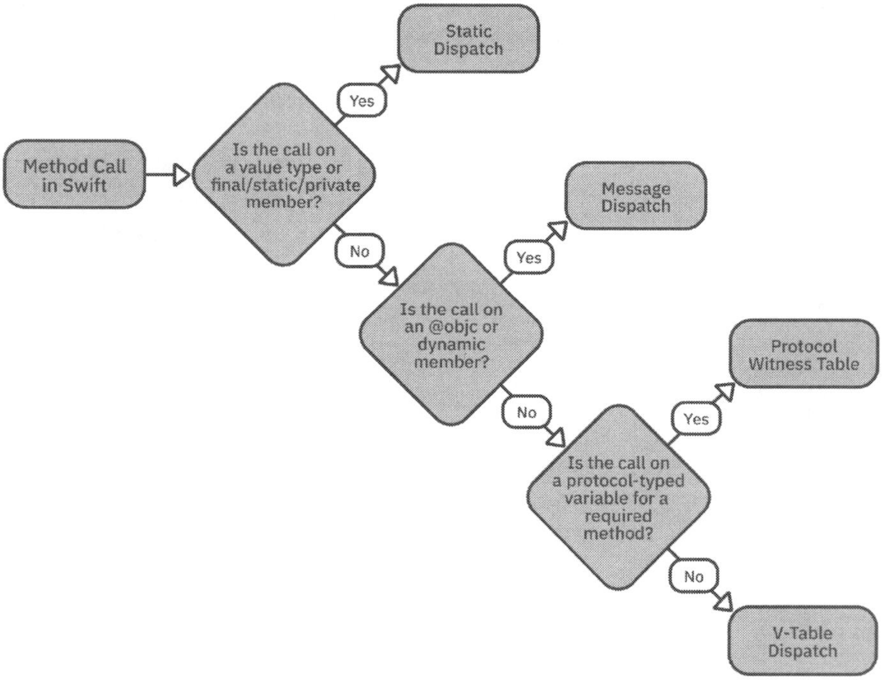

Flow chart showing dispatch after a method call

Dispatch Types: Comparison Table

Here is a small table showing the main differences between the dispatch types:

Type	Speed	Common Use Cases
Static Dispatch	Fastest	Value types, final/fileprivate/private/ static methods
V-Table Dispatch	Fast	Inheritance, overridable class methods
Protocol Witness Table	Medium	Protocols with required methods
Message Dispatch	Slowest	`@objc`, KVO, `#selector`, Obj-C interop

A quick comparison between dispatch types

Existential a.k.a Boxed Type Protocol

An existential is when you use `any Protocol` as a type in Swift. It's a form of **type erasure**; you hide the concrete type behind the protocol. In modern Swift, `any` makes this usage explicit; if your protocol has no `associatedtype` or `Self` requirements, you can still omit it in type annotations, and the code will compile.

You use an existential when you don't know the type at compile time, and at runtime, it could be *anything* that conforms to the protocol. This gives you flexibility: you can pass around "anything that logs" without caring *how* it logs.

Swift stores the value in an existential container and calls methods via the protocol witness table, resulting in dynamic dispatch.

If the value fits in the existential container's inline buffer, Swift stores it there; otherwise, it stores a pointer to a heap allocation. Either way, existential types use dynamic dispatch, which is slower than static dispatch.

associatedtype: A placeholder type within a protocol, where the actual type is determined by the conforming concrete type. This enhances the protocol's flexibility, allowing it to adapt to various use cases.

Check the example below:

```
protocol Logger {
  func log(_ message: String)
}

struct ConsoleLogger: Logger {
  func log(_ message: String) {
    print("Writing to console: \(message)")
  }
}

struct FileLogger: Logger {
  func log(_ message: String) {
    print("Writing to file: \(message)")
  }
}
```

Now you pass around the existential as a type, like:

```
func runLogger(_ logger: any Logger) { // 'any' is optional here
  logger.log("Hello from an existential Logger!")
}

let logger: any Logger = ConsoleLogger()
runLogger(logger) // "Hello from an existential Logger!"
```

It works perfectly, even if you don't know what concrete type might be coming in the logger.

If your protocols require `associatedtype` or `Self`, then you can't directly use it as an existential type. Look at this code:

```
protocol Logger {
  associatedtype Message
  func log(_ message: Message)
}
```

Now, if you do this:

```
let logger: Logger = ConsoleLogger() // Use of protocol 'Logger'
as a type must be written 'any Logger'
```

You fix it by adding `any`:

```
let logger: any Logger = ConsoleLogger()
```

The code compiles now, but there's another catch — `runLogger()` will throw this error:

```
func runLogger(_ logger: any Logger) {
  logger.log("Hello from an existential Logger!") // Member
'log' cannot be used on value of type 'any Logger'; consider
using a generic constraint instead
}
```

That's because the compiler doesn't know the concrete type of the associated type at compile time. After all, it's erased.

You can think of this error message as the compiler saying, "I have trust issues." It's aware that you *probably* mean well, but since you erased the type, it prevents you from accessing the associated data. It's not being mean, it's just being very, very careful.

But if your protocol method doesn't take the associated type as a parameter, like this:

```
protocol Logger {
  associatedtype Message
  func placeHolder() -> Message
}

struct ConsoleLogger: Logger {
  // ...
  func placeHolder() -> String {
    "Writing to console:"
  }
}

func printLoggerPlaceHolder(_ logger: any Logger) {
  print(logger.placeHolder()) // Compiles, without error
}
```

This compiles fine, but why? The call compiles because the *usage* of the return value doesn't require the compiler to know the concrete type of `Message`. The `print()` method takes an argument of type `Any`, and any value can be converted to `Any`. The compiler doesn't need to know if `Message` is a `String` or an `Int`; it just knows it's *some value* that it can pass to `print()`.

> **Pro Tip**: Be explicit with types whenever possible. It avoids unnecessary runtime work and can make your code run faster.

When to Use Existential Types?

Here are some of the most common cases where existential types shine:

- **Heterogeneous Collections**: When you want to store instances of unrelated objects that conform to the same protocol.For example, you have an `AppsFlyerTracker` and an `AdjustTracker` that conform to the `Tracker` protocol.

```
protocol Tracker {
  func track(_ key: String, parameters: [String: Any])
}

struct AppsFlyerTracker: Tracker {
  func track(_ key: String, parameters: [String : Any]) {
    // some AppsFlyer tracking code.
  }
}

struct AdjustTracker: Tracker {
  func track(_ key: String, parameters: [String : Any]) {
    // some Adjust tracking code.
  }
}
```

You can store them in an array like:

```
let trackers: [any Tracker] = [AppsFlyerTracker(),
AdjustTracker()]
```

And then use them interchangeably:

```
for tracker in trackers {
  tracker.track("some_event", parameters: ["some_key":
"some_value"])
}
```

- **SwiftUI's `any View`:** A common SwiftUI pattern. Suppose you have one view that displays a list of user data, and another that shows an empty state.

```
func showRelevantView(_ hasNoUserData: Bool) -> any View {
  hasNoUserData ? UserDataView() : EmptyStateView()
}
```

Trade-offs: Always remember that existentials come with costs: performance overhead from dynamic dispatch and the loss of compile-time type information. Using any indiscriminately is like ordering the *Surprise Special* at a restaurant. Sure, it's flexible, but you pay extra for it and might end up with something heavy that takes a long time to digest (because of dynamic dispatch overhead).

Opaque Types

This is another way Swift hides the concrete type from the outside world. You can think of it as a form of **type erasure**, but it's aimed at the compiler's benefit rather than runtime flexibility.

The key difference from `any` is that with `some`, the compiler still knows the concrete type at compile time, so it can skip the existential container and generate more optimized code. You still get abstraction in your API, but without paying the boxing cost you get with existentials.

Here's a working example:

```
protocol Logger {
  func log(_ message: String)
}

struct ConsoleLogger: Logger {
  func log(_ message: String) {
    print("[LOG]: \(message)")
  }
}

func makeLogger() -> some Logger {
  ConsoleLogger()
}

let logger = makeLogger()
logger.log("Hello from an opaque return type!")
```

The `some` keyword in `makeLogger()` makes the return type *opaque*.From the caller's perspective, they only know it's "something that conforms to `Logger`." They don't know (or care) that it's a `ConsoleLogger`.

Opaque types are like that friend who says, "I know a guy who can fix your car." When you ask, "Who is it?" they just say, "Don't worry about it. It's a mechanic you can *trust*." You don't get the name, but you get the guarantee that the car will be fixed.

`some` avoids the existential container, but it doesn't magically make everything *statically* dispatched. It guarantees that for a given method call, one specific concrete type is always returned because:

1. The compiler knows this single concrete type at the call site, it can perform significant optimizations.
2. If the concrete type is a `struct`, `enum`, or a `final class`, the compiler can often devirtualize the call and dispatch it statically. This is a major performance win.
3. If the concrete type is a non-final `class`, the method call will be dispatched dynamically through the class's v-table, not the protocol's witness table.
4. The PWT is involved at compile time to ensure the type conforms, but the runtime dispatch can often be more direct (static or v-table) than the PWT-based dispatch required by an existential `any`.

> **Devirtualization**:A compiler optimization technique that replaces a slower dynamic method call with a faster, direct method call.

some vs any

Take a look at the following comparison between `some` and `any`:

Feature	some	any
Primary Use Case	Hiding a specific concrete return type from an API caller (abstraction).	Storing different concrete types that conform to the same protocol in a heterogeneous collection.
Existential container	Does *not* use an existential container — compiler knows the type.	Always uses an existential container (stores witness table + value).
PWT for protocol requirements	Uses the protocol witness table for requirement calls.	Also uses the protocol witness table.
Extra indirection	Directly stores the value or reference.	Always adds an extra layer of indirection through existential storage.
Static dispatch	For non-requirement extension methods (always static).	For non-requirement extension methods (always static).
Memory layout	Fixed and known at compile time.	Unknown at compile time.

some vs. any

Uncommon Dispatch Scenarios

At this point, you might think you know everything about dispatch, but Swift can surprise you in different situations. Dispatch sometimes behaves the opposite of what you expect. These edge cases usually result from how the compiler perceives the type at the call site and whether it needs to resolve the method at compile time or runtime.

Let's explore some less common but important cases.

The dynamic Keyword

If you mark a method as `dynamic` even if you aren't using it with Objective-C or any Objective-C runtime features, Swift defers its resolution until runtime. Check the following snippet:

```
class Example: NSObject {
  dynamic func greet() {
    print("Hello")
  }
}
```

Even if the method could have been resolved with v-table dispatch, it will now be forced to use message dispatch, adding overhead.

Chained Dispatch

In some scenarios, you may encounter a situation where both an existential container and a PWT lookup occur.Example:

```
func callLog<T: Logger>(_ logger: T) where T: AnyObject { // 1
  let existential: any Logger = logger // 2
  existential.log("Hello") // 3
}
```

Here's the chain:

1. Generic dispatch to get into `callLog()` (static).
2. Creating an existential.
3. PWT lookup to call `log()`.

This is rare, but if you accidentally introduce existential inside generic contexts, you lose some of the generics' performance benefits.

Static Dispatch Isn't Always Inline

It's incorrect to assume that the compiler always inlines static dispatch methods. That's not always true. Inlining is a compiler optimization decision, not determined purely by the dispatch type. Therefore, the compiler might choose not to inline a large method.

SwiftUI and Dispatch

Since the release of SwiftUI, you can see how much static dispatch is happening behind the scenes — for one reason: performance. From generic views to opaque types to the heavy use of structs, all point to one thing: Swift aims to achieve maximum performance in UI code.

Class Methods vs. Static Methods

In classes, you can have both class and static type methods, but their dispatch behaviors differ.

- A `static func` on a class is implicitly `final`. It cannot be overridden by a subclass and is always called using static dispatch.
- A `class func` can be overridden by subclasses. It executes using dynamic dispatch through the v-table.

```
class Vehicle {
  static func vehicleType() -> String {
    return "Generic Vehicle"
  }

  class func maxSpeed() -> Int {
    return 100
  }
}

class Car: Vehicle {
  // SUCCESS: Can override class method
  override class func maxSpeed() -> Int {
    return 250
  }
}

// Static Dispatch: The compiler calls Vehicle.vehicleType()
directly.
print(Car.vehicleType()) // Prints: "Generic Vehicle"

// Dynamic Dispatch: The compiler does a v-table lookup to find
Car's implementation.
print(Car.maxSpeed()) // Prints: "250"
```

The key takeaway is that `static` guarantees a single implementation for better performance, while `class` allows for polymorphic behavior at the type level.

Inheritance and Protocol Conformance

Have you considered what occurs when a subclass overrides a method that is also required by a protocol? Does Swift use the v-table or the PWT? The answer is: both, in a sense.

Take a look at the following code:

```
protocol Heatable {
  func heat()
}

class Appliance: Heatable {
  func heat() {
    print("The appliance is heating up.")
  }
}

class Toaster: Appliance {
  override func heat() { // 1
    print("The toaster is toasting bread.")
  }
}

let heater: any Heatable = Toaster() // 2
heater.heat() // Prints: "The toaster is toasting bread."
```

Breaking down the code above:

1. `Toaster` overrides the `heat()` method from its superclass `Appliance`.
2. You store a `Toaster` instance in an existential `any Heatable`.

When `heater.heat()` is called, here's what happens:

1. The call involves an existential question, so Swift begins a PWT lookup to find the implementation of `heat()` for `Toaster`.
2. The PWT entry for a class method doesn't point directly to the implementation. Instead, it points to a small adapter function (a thunk) that then performs a v-table lookup.
3. The v-table lookup correctly resolves to the most specific implementation, which is the `override` in the `Toaster` subclass.

This ensures class inheritance and method overriding work correctly, even when the object is wrapped inside a protocol existential.

Generics vs Existentials

It's one of Swift's most powerful features. It helps you achieve reusability, flexibility, and type safety. With this, you can write code that avoids duplication.

Swift's `Array`, `Dictionary`, and `Set` are generic collections. You can also create your own custom generic types in Swift.

Swift allows you to create custom types if needed. Check out the following:

```
struct Queue<Element> {
  private var elements: [Element]

  init(elements: [Element]) {
    self.elements = elements
  }

  mutating func enqueue(_ element: Element) {
    self.elements.append(element)
  }

  mutating func dequeue() -> Element? {
    guard !elements.isEmpty else { return nil }
    return elements.removeFirst()
  }
}
```

The code above shows you how to write a generic queue. Now, if you were to do:

```
var idsQueue = Queue<Int>(elements: []) // A queue of Ids
idsQueue.enqueue(1)
idsQueue.enqueue(2)

var peopleQueue = Queue<String>(elements: []) // A queue of
People
peopleQueue.enqueue("Steve")
peopleQueue.enqueue("Jobs")
```

The code above demonstrates reusability. You can use the same code for `Int`, `String`, or any other types that Swift provides.

Generics may seem similar to Existentials, but they are entirely different. Generics are more aware of the type during compile time. You can think of them as: "Tell me exactly which type you'll use, and I'll optimize for it." Meanwhile, with Existentials, it's runtime-based, more like: "It could be anything, I'll figure it out later."

Consider the following example:

```
protocol Animal {
  func sleep()
}

class Dog: Animal {
  func sleep() {
    print("Dog is sleeping.")
  }
}

func makeItSleep<T: Animal>(_ animal: T) {
  animal.sleep()
}
```

When the compiler encounters a call to a generic method like `makeItSleep(myDog)`, it generates a specialized version of that method for the Dog type - almost as if you had written `makeItSleep_Dog(_ animal: Dog)`.

1. Within this specialized method, the compiler knows the exact type is Dog
2. Since `Dog` is a class, the `sleep()` method call is dispatched through its v-table.
3. If you had called this function with a struct conforming to `Animal`, the specialized method would use static dispatch because the implementation is known at compile time.

Generics behave more like opaque types than like existential types. Both preserve type information at compile time; the key difference is who controls the concrete type.

A generic parameter and an opaque type parameter serve a similar purpose — both allow callers to supply any concrete type that satisfies a constraint.

However, a **generic return type** is set by the caller's context and can resolve to any type that satisfies the constraint. On the other hand, an **opaque return type** can only be one specific concrete implementation, while hiding the type from outside visibility.

Protocol Composition

Sometimes, you may want a type to conform to multiple protocols. Protocol composition lets you express this by using the & operator.

Think of it as:

> **I don't care what you are, as long as you can do *this* and *that*.**

Here is a quick example:

```
protocol Flyable {
  func fly()
}

protocol Swimmable {
  func swim()
}

struct Duck: Flyable, Swimmable {
  func fly() { print("Flapping wings!") }
  func swim() { print("Paddling in the pond!") }
}

func makeItMove(_ creature: Flyable & Swimmable) { // 1
  creature.fly() // 2
  creature.swim() // 3
}

makeItMove(Duck()) // 4
```

So, what exactly is going on here?

1. The protocol composition of `Flyable` & `Swimmable`.
2. `fly()` is available.
3. Because of the protocol composition, the method `swim()` is also available.
4. Prints:

- Flapping wings!
- Paddling in the pond!

Protocol composition does not merge methods into a new type. Instead, it acts as a type constraint that enforces conformance to all listed protocols.

Dispatch works as if you were calling methods from each protocol separately.

Additionally, you can specify protocol composition with either `any` or `some` to enforce an existential or opaque type.

> **Tip**: When creating a protocol composition with many protocols, it's better to define a protocol that inherits from all of them to keep your code organized and clean.

Common Pitfalls

Even if you've been writing Swift for many years, it's easy to stumble into subtle traps that protocols and dispatch can cause. Some of these incorrect behaviors and reduced performance may leave you scratching your head, wondering why they behave a certain way, why the compiler won't let you do something that seems perfectly reasonable.

Below, you'll go through the common traps programmers often get stuck in.

Default Methods in Protocol Extensions

The default implementation using extensions is a powerful way to leverage Swift's flexibility. However, extensions behave differently in certain scenarios.

1. If you provide a default implementation for a protocol requirement method, then the conforming type's implementation executes each time.
2. If the method exists only in the extension and not in the protocol definition, then the compiler uses the extended version, even when a conforming type implements it.

```
protocol Greeter {
  func greet()
}

extension Greeter {
  func greet() { print("Hello from default!") }
}

struct Person: Greeter {
  func greet() { print("Hello from Person!") }
}
```

```
let john = Person()
john.greet() // Hello from Person!

let greeter: Greeter = Person()
greeter.greet() // Hello from Person!
```

But watch this twist:

```
protocol Greeter {}

extension Greeter {
  func greet() { print("Hello from default!") }
}

struct Person: Greeter {
  func greet() { print("Hello from Person!") }
}

let greeter: Greeter = Person()
greeter.greet() // Hello from default!
```

This happens because `greet()` isn't a protocol requirement, so existential calls are statically dispatched to the default method.

If you want the version from the conforming type to be used *dynamically*, do one of the following:

1. Make the method a protocol requirement.
2. Use the concrete type directly rather than the protocol existential.

Existentials with associatedtype

Even though Swift now allows you to create existentials with protocols having `associatedtype` or `Self`, an existential removes the type information tied to the associated type, which means you cannot directly call methods that depend on it.

Take a look at the following snippet:

```
protocol Logger {
  associatedtype Message
  func log(_ message: Message)
}

func testLogger(_ logger: any Logger) {
  logger.log("Hello") // Error – Message type is erased
}
```

To make it work, you can:

Option 1: Use generics so the compiler preserves the type:

```
func testLogger<T: Logger>(_ logger: T, message: T.Message) {
  logger.log(message)
}
```

Option 2: Type-erase manually with something like `AnyLogger`.

It's easy to forget this subtle point, which can lead to perfectly valid-looking code that doesn't compile.

Guide your Compiler

Don't let your compiler struggle with simple tasks; guide it where possible. If you're not using existentials, opt for opaque types instead.

Don't do this:

```
func makeLogger() -> any Logger {
  ConsoleLogger()
}
```

Prefer this:

```
func makeLogger() -> some Logger {
  ConsoleLogger()
}
```

It seems like a small change, but for the compiler, it's a significant performance advantage. It not only accelerates the program but also enables more compile-time checks.

Most pitfalls come down to one idea:

> **What does the compiler know at compile time, and what must it resolve at runtime?**

If you can recognize when type information is maintained or erased, and when dispatch is static or dynamic, you can avoid silent performance issues and unexpected behaviors.

Once you develop the habit of thinking this way before writing code, you'll stop just "using Swift" and start bending Swift to your will.

Key Points

- Protocols facilitate polymorphism for classes and value types, enabling shared behavior without inheritance.
- Default method implementations in protocol extensions can minimize boilerplate but may also lead to subtle differences in dispatch behavior.
- Conditional conformance lets a type conform to a protocol only when certain compile-time constraints are met.
- Static dispatch happens for value types, final classes, and private/fileprivate/static methods, allowing compile-time inlining.
- Dynamic dispatch is used when the specific implementation is unknown until runtime, and it occurs in various forms.
- V-table dispatch enables method overriding in class inheritance by referencing the method pointer in a virtual table.
- An existential container occurs when assigning a concrete value to a protocol-typed variable that stores metadata, the value, and the witness table pointer.
- The PWT links each protocol requirement to its specific implementation, facilitating method resolution for existentials.
- V-table dispatch works directly with class inheritance; PWT dispatch introduces existential container indirection, making it slightly slower.
- Message dispatch via the Objective-C runtime enables features like `#selector`, **KVO**, and **method swizzling**, and is the slowest form of dispatch.
- The `dynamic` keyword enforces Objective-C style message dispatch even when v-table dispatch could be used.
- Opaque types can hide the specific type from the caller while still allowing the compiler to identify it at compile time for optimization.

- Existentials (`any`) conceal the concrete type from both the caller and compiler, requiring PWT-based dispatch at runtime.
- `some` vs. `any`: Both use PWT for protocol requirements, but `some` avoid existential containers and can be inlined more often.
- Generics are resolved at compile time, avoiding boxing and enabling specialization; existentials are resolved at runtime.
- Protocol composition (`A & B`) enforces multiple constraints without creating a new type, and it works with both `any` and `some`.
- Default methods in extensions that are not required use static dispatch for existential calls, even if a conforming type implements them.
- Existentials with `associatedtype` or `Self` lose compile-time type information, preventing direct calls to dependent methods.
- Manual type erasure (e.g., `AnyLogger`) can regain flexibility when protocols with `associatedtype` need to be stored as existentials.
- Always consider what the compiler knows at compile time versus runtime to avoid hidden dispatch costs.

Challenge

AnyLogger Wrapper: Existential & Generic Versions

Create a wrapper called `AnyLogger` that can accept any type conforming to the `Logger` protocol defined earlier in the chapter. Your task is to implement two versions: one using an Existential, and the other using Generics.

Requirement

1. Your `Logger` protocol should include at least one method: `log(_ message: String)`.
2. `AnyLogger` should work with both `ConsoleLogger` and `FileLogger` without modifying their implementations.

Example Usage

```
let consoleLogger = ConsoleLogger()
let fileLogger = FileLogger()

// Existential version
let anyExistentialLogger: AnyLogger = AnyLogger(consoleLogger)
anyExistentialLogger.log("Hello Existential!")

// Generic version
let anyGenericLogger = AnyLogger(consoleLogger) // Generic<T:
Logger>
anyGenericLogger.log("Hello Generic!")
```

Let the logger game begin!

Where to Go From Here?

Now that you've explored dispatch, existentials, opaque types, and generics, you should have a clear understanding of how they operate and behave in different scenarios.

This chapter not only guided you through practical examples but also aimed to shape how you think about writing code in real-world situations.

The goal is to help you intentionally choose the right approach for each case, so you can write code that is not only correct but also high-performing and optimized.

Chapter 3: Metamorphosis: Ars Generalis

Aaqib Hussain

The term "algorithm" is a Latinization of the name of the 9th-century Persian mathematician **Muhammad ibn Musa Al-Khwarizmi**, the *father of algebra*. His work was revolutionary because it established abstract rules for solving entire classes of problems, rather than just individual equations. He taught the world to think in patterns.

That same leap from a specific number to an abstract variable is the core idea behind modern programming. Where Al-Khwarizmi used a symbol like *x* (not a literal x but a variant of it from the Persian alphabet) to represent any number, Swift uses generics (like `<T>`) to represent any type.

In this chapter, you will adopt that same mindset. You will master Swift's generic system to create powerful, abstract blueprints, such as reusable parsers and type-safe network requests, that solve entire classes of programming problems with elegant, reusable solutions.

> **Reliable software resides in scalable architecture and a well-defined codebase.**

Designing with Generic Protocols

By this point, you already understand how associated types work. Now, it's time to apply that knowledge and delve deeper into the architecture side of things. Knowing *what* a tool is and knowing *how* to use it are completely different skills. In this section, you'll use generic protocols to create systems that are flexible, abstract, and safe.

You'll begin by consolidating repetitive concrete protocols into a single reusable generic blueprint. Then you'll design protocols with multiple associated types, and finally, learn how to enforce rules on the blueprints themselves.

Moving from Concrete to Abstract

Writing great architecture is all about identifying common patterns and minimizing duplication. Now imagine you're building an app that needs to fetch different kinds of data. You might begin by defining a protocol for each kind.

```
protocol UserDataSource {
  func fetchUsers() -> [User]
}

protocol ProductDataSource {
  func fetchProducts() -> [Product]
}
```

This works, but you've already created a problem. The core logic, which involves fetching a list of items, is the same. If you later add a `TransactionDataSource`, you'll end up copying and pasting the same idea again. This shows that you're working with concrete details rather than abstract patterns.

The solution is to create a single, generic blueprint that models the data-fetching pattern. By using `associatedtype`, you can define a unified protocol to manage them all.

```
protocol DataSource {
  associatedtype Item
  func fetchItems() -> [Item]
}
```

Now, a UserDataSource simply implements DataSource and specifies its Item as User. This isn't just about saving a few lines of code; it's a conceptual leap. You've established a unified abstraction for a broad class of problems, enabling you to create other components that can work with any DataSource, regardless of the specific item it provides.

At this point, you might be wondering, "What is happening here? I still need to implement fetchItems() methods for both UserDataSource and ProductDataSource." You are right to think that.

This becomes valuable when consuming these data sources. Consider if you were to pass them around. You would have no choice but to inject both like this:

```
func displayUserCount(from source: UserDataSource) {
  let count = source.fetchUsers().count
  print("There are \(count) users.")
}

func displayProductCount(from source: ProductDataSource) {
  let count = source.fetchProducts().count
  print("There are \(count) products.")
}
```

Here, you've duplicated the logic in displayUserCount() and displayProductCount(). If you add a TransactionDataSource, you'll need to write a third function, displayTransactionCount(). This code is fragile, repetitive, and doesn't scale well.

Introducing DataSource here solves this problem. You can pass it around like this:

```
struct User {
  // ... Some properties
}

struct UserDataSourceImpl: DataSource {
  typealias Item = User

  func fetchItems() -> [User] {
    [User()]
  }
}

struct Product {
  // ... Some properties
}

struct ProductDataSourceImpl: DataSource {
  typealias Item = Product
```

```
  func fetchItems() -> [Product] {
    [Product()]
  }
}

func displayItemCount<S: DataSource>(from source: S) {
  let count = source.fetchItems().count
  print("There are \(count) items of type \(S.Item.self).")
}
```

This single generic function removes duplication, allowing it to work with any `DataSource` while ensuring compile-time type safety.

Designing with Multiple Associated Types

A generic protocol doesn't mean it can only have one associated type. For more complex interactions, it can include multiple associated types to create a comprehensive, descriptive contract that guarantees type safety across several related types. A real-world example of this pattern is a network request layer.

A network request typically includes several key components: a path, an HTTP method, an optional request body, and a specific response type you expect to receive. Something like:

```
enum HTTPMethod: String {
  case post
  case get
}

protocol APIRequest {
  associatedtype RequestBody: Encodable
  associatedtype Response: Decodable

  var path: String { get }
  var method: HTTPMethod { get }
}
```

Here, the `RequestBody` represents the encodable data you send with the request, and `Response` represents the decodable type you expect to receive.

To implement a specific request to a particular endpoint, you create a struct conforming to this protocol. For example, creating a request would look something like this:

```
struct User: Encodable {
  // ... Some properties
}
```

```
struct UserConfirmation: Decodable {
  // ... Some properties
}

struct CreateUserRequest: APIRequest {
  typealias RequestBody = User
  typealias Response = UserConfirmation

  let path = "/users"
  let method: HTTPMethod = .post
  let newUser: User
}
```

This pattern is incredibly powerful. It creates a collection of lightweight, strongly typed request objects. A generic networking client can accept any object conforming to `APIRequest` with compile-time certainty about which type to encode and which to decode. This eliminates the common pitfall of accidentally decoding the wrong model from an API response.

> **Note**: You cannot have an optional associated type. You must either provide an empty type or omit that associated type from the protocol entirely.

Constraining Associated Types in the Protocol Definition

While the `where` clause is one way to constrain a protocol, you can also apply constraints directly to associated types within a protocol's definition using protocol composition. This approach enforces a rule on the blueprint itself, requiring that any conforming type must use a type that meets specific criteria.

Revisiting the `DataSource` protocol, imagine you need a guarantee that any item fetched from a data source can be uniquely identified and compared for equality. You can enforce this by constraining the `Item` associated type directly to the combination of `Identifiable & Equatable`.

```
protocol DataSource {
  associatedtype Item: Identifiable & Equatable
  func fetchItems() -> [Item]
}
```

With this, the `DataSource` protocol shifts from being a friendly host to a strict nightclub bouncer. It stands at the door and says, "Sorry, your Item isn't Identifiable or Equatable. You're not on the list." The compiler becomes your enforcer, catching troublemakers long before they can cause issues at runtime.

```
struct UserDataSourceImpl: DataSource { // Error: Type
'UserDataSourceImpl' does not conform to protocol 'DataSource'
  typealias Item = User

  func fetchItems() -> [User] {
    [User()]
  }
}
struct ProductDataSourceImpl: DataSource { // Error: Type
'ProductDataSourceImpl' does not conform to protocol
'DataSource'
  typealias Item = Product

  func fetchItems() -> [Product] {
    [Product()]
  }
}
```

This approach is fundamental to designing robust, self-documenting protocols. It shifts the responsibility of meeting requirements onto the conforming type, and catches potential errors at compile time, making the abstraction safer and more explicit about its needs.

Constraining Abstractions: The where Clause

An abstraction without rules is chaotic; an abstraction with well-defined rules is powerful.

In Swift, the `where` clause is one of those tools that help enforce rules for generic protocols and functions. It allows adding constraints beyond basic syntax, ensuring the code is not only flexible but also fundamentally safe.

Pattern 1: Constraining an Associated Type

The `where` clause is often used to apply constraints to an associated type in a protocol. This allows you to write generic methods that work with specific types (like `DataSource`), provided their nested associated type (`Item`) meets certain requirements.

Now revisit the `DataSource` protocol. Imagine you want to create a single generic method that checks if a data source contains a particular item. For this, the associated type must be `Equatable`.

You face a design choice: should you require all `DataSource` instances to have `Equatable` items by constraining the protocol, or should this requirement apply only to the specific method?

For maximum reusability, the latter is better. That's where the `where` clause comes in handy to apply this local rule.

```
protocol DataSource {
  associatedtype Item
  func fetchItems() -> [Item]
}

func dataSource<S: DataSource>(contains item: S.Item, in source:
S) -> Bool where S.Item: Equatable {
  return source.fetchItems().contains(item)
}
```

Here's a breakdown of the signature:

1. `<S: DataSource>` sets the primary constraint.
2. The `where S.Item: Equatable` clause adds a temporary, specific rule for this method only.

This informs the compiler: "Only allow calls to this method when the `Item` type of `S` conforms to `Equatable`."

This approach combines the best of both worlds: the `DataSource` protocol remains simple and widely applicable, while the `dataSource(contains:in:)` method is assured to be type-safe without enforcing a permanent restriction on the protocol itself.

Pattern 2: Matching Two Associated Types

You can use the `where` clause to ensure the associated types of two different generic parameters are the same. This is useful for writing methods that manage interactions between distinct but related generic types, like a network response and a local cache.

Consider an API that provides a list of users and a local cache that stores them. You want to write a single generic method that identifies which API users are not yet in the cache. This comparison is only possible if both the API and the cache operate on the same item type.

The protocol definitions might look like this. Note that the items must be `Hashable` to perform an efficient diff using a `Set`.

```
protocol APIResponse {
  associatedtype Item: Hashable
  var items: [Item] { get }
}

protocol DataCache {
  associatedtype Item: Hashable
  func getCachedItems() -> Set<Item>
}
```

Now, you can write a generic function that is guaranteed to be safe.

```
func findNewItems<Response: APIResponse, Cache: DataCache>(
  in response: Response,
  comparedTo cache: Cache
) -> Set<Response.Item> where Response.Item == Cache.Item {
  let freshItems = Set(response.items)
  let cachedItems = cache.getCachedItems()
  return freshItems.subtracting(cachedItems)
}
```

The key here is the `where Response.Item == Cache.Item` clause. It instructs the compiler to allow this method only when both associated types match.

Here's an example of how it behaves:

```
struct UserResponse: APIResponse {
  typealias Item = User
  var items: [User] = []
}

struct UserDataCache: DataCache {
  typealias Item = User
```

```
    func getCachedItems() -> Set<User> {
      // Some user list
      return ...
    }
}

struct ProductDataCache: DataCache {
    typealias Item = Product

    func getCachedItems() -> Set<Product> {
      // Some product list
      return ....
    }
}
findNewItems(in: UserResponse(), comparedTo: ProductDataCache())
// Global function 'findNewItems(in:comparedTo:)' requires the
types 'UserResponse.Item' (aka 'User') and
'ProductDataCache.Item' (aka 'Product') be equivalent
```

As you can see, the compiler immediately stops the build. The `where` clause prevents accidental comparisons between `User` and `Product`. This is the power of compile-time safety; the bug is caught before the app can run.

The Compiler's Secret: Generic Specialization

The question now is how Swift manages complexity without compromising performance. You might think that such high-level abstractions could lead to increased runtime costs, but in Swift, that's rarely the case.

This isn't just magic: it's a complex compiler technique called **generic specialization**. Understanding this process is key to appreciating why generics are not only a tool for abstraction but also for writing extremely fast code. You'll now examine how the compiler converts your abstract blueprints into highly optimized machine code.

How the Compiler Creates Specialized Code

At its core, specialization is the process by which the compiler takes a generic method and generates distinct, concrete versions of it for each type for which it's used.

Here is an analogy to understand it better:

Imagine you're a blacksmith in medieval times with a master blueprint for a sword. When a knight comes to you and asks for a steel longsword, you follow the blueprint to craft that specific sword out of steel. When a royal guard requests a ceremonial bronze shortsword, you use the same blueprint to create a completely different, specialized sword out of bronze. The blueprint is generic; the swords it produces are specialized.

In that way, the Swift compiler is like that blacksmith. Consider the generic function:

```
func printAndReturn<T>(_ value: T) -> T {
  print("Value: \(value)")
  return value
}
```

When you call this function with different types in your code:

```
let number = printAndReturn(101)        // Called with Int
let text = printAndReturn("Bears. Beets. Battlestar Galactica")
// Called with String
```

At compile time, Swift does not keep generic <T> versions around. Instead, it creates two specialized, non-generic versions of the function behind the scenes, almost as if you had manually written these:

```
func printAndReturn_Int(_ value: Int) -> Int {
  print("Value: \(value)")
  return value
}

func printAndReturn_String(_ value: String) -> String {
  print("Value: \(value)")
  return value
}
```

Because these versions are created at compile time, the compiler knows the exact memory layout and can perform extensive optimizations.

Devirtualization: From Dynamic to Static Dispatch

Devirtualization is a powerful result of specialization that directly relates to the method dispatch concepts introduced in Chapter 2. When you use a protocol as an existential type like `any SomeProtocol`, the compiler doesn't know the concrete type at runtime. To call a method, it must perform a dynamic dispatch, which adds a small but real layer of overhead.

However, generics change this situation entirely.

Check the following code:

```
func processItems<C: Collection>(_ items: C) {
  print("Processing \(items.count) items.")
}

let userIDs: [Int] = [101, 102, 103]
let productCategories: Set<String> = ["Bears", "Beets",
"Battlestar Galactica"]
processItems(userIDs)
processItems(productCategories)
```

When the compiler sees these calls, it generates specialized versions of `processItems` for both `Array<Int>` and `Set<String>`. Inside the specialized version for the `productCategories` call, the compiler knows with complete certainty that items is a `Set<String>` and not just some abstract Collection.

To picture how the compiler separates a single generic definition into distinct, optimized implementations, consider the following illustration:

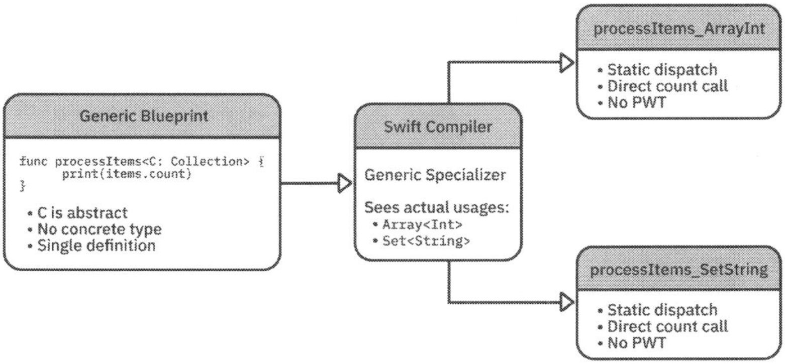

The Generic Specialization Process: From Abstract to Concrete

This knowledge is a compiler superpower. It bypasses the Protocol Witness Table entirely and replaces the dynamic lookup for a property, such as `.count`, with a direct, hardcoded call to `Set.count`.

This transformation from dynamic dispatch to static dispatch is known as devirtualization. It's one of Swift's most important optimizations and a major reason why generics almost always outperform existentials. With generics, you can write high-level, elegant abstractions without sacrificing runtime performance.

The Performance Trade-Offs of Generics

Specialization dramatically improves runtime performance, but it comes with a trade-off: increased binary size.

This happens because the compiler creates a separate, specialized copy of your generic function for each unique concrete type you use, which causes your final binary to become larger. For example, if you have a single generic function used with 50 different types throughout your app, there will be 50 different machine code copies of that function in your final executable.

For most apps, this trade-off is reasonable. The increase in binary size is usually negligible compared to the benefits of faster runtime and better type safety. It's essential to remember that the cost of a generic is paid during compile time and affects binary size, not at runtime.

Escaping the Existential Box: Working with PATs

Now that you understand how generics work and why they are fast, you can reason about the "existential crisis" caused by protocols with associated types (PATs). In Chapter 2, you saw that using a PAT as an existential type threw a compile error. In this section, you'll learn exactly why that happened and how to resolve it.

You will now cover two powerful solutions: the highly performant, generic approach that leverages compiler specialization, and the type-erasure pattern for situations that demand greater flexibility. Mastering these patterns is the key to unlocking the full architectural power of protocols in Swift.

The PAT Problem Revisited: Why It Fails

The problem with PATs arises when you use them in a `Collection` or any variable.

Looking back at the example from Chapter 2:

```
func runLogger(_ logger: any Logger) {
  logger.log("Hello from an existential Logger!") // Member
'log' cannot be used on value of type 'any Logger'; consider
using a generic constraint instead
}
```

The compiler stops here with an error message.

The reason for this error is the lack of information. When the compiler sees a type like `any Logger`, it has no idea of the concrete type because the type has been removed. It can only guess at it. Without knowing the concrete type and its memory layout, the compiler cannot allocate the correct amount of storage for a variable like **logger**. Furthermore, it can't guarantee type safety for any method calls involving the associated type.

The High-Performance Generic Approach

The compiler's error message itself provides the best solution: "consider using a generic constraint instead". This should be the default whenever possible, as it is both the simplest and most efficient way to address the problem. Instead of trying to force a PAT into an existential box, you retain the type information by making the code that uses it generic.

If you go back to the earlier example:

```
func runLogger(_ logger: any Logger) {
  logger.log("Hello from an existential Logger!") // Member
'log' cannot be used on value of type 'any Logger'; consider
using a generic constraint instead
}
```

However, the generic approach works perfectly:

```
func runLogger<T: Logger>(_ logger: T, message: T.Message) where
T.Message == String {
  logger.log(message)
}
```

When you use `<T: Logger>`, the compiler specializes your code. It generates a unique `runLogger` instance for each `Logger` type. This enables devirtualization, leading to fast static dispatch. You can keep your code abstract and high-level, and the compiler still ensures it runs efficiently.

The Architecture of Type Erasure: Deconstructing the Pattern

The generic approach is the ideal solution and works in most cases, but what if you need to pass around "any logger" as a parameter or store different kinds of loggers in a single collection? For these situations, you must turn to type erasure.

The purpose of type erasure is to hide the complex details of a protocol, such as its associated types, from the public-facing API by wrapping them in a concrete type. You'll create your own concrete struct, `AnyLogger`, which manages the complexity internally while presenting a simple, uniform interface.

Type Erasure Explained

To be able to call the `log(_ message: Message)` on `any Logger`, you would need to hide the `associatedtype` from the compiler. This can be done by creating a wrapper `AnyLogger`. The next challenge is how a single `AnyLogger` wrapper can hold onto any possible `Logger`.

Instead of storing the concrete logger directly in the struct AnyLogger, you'll store a reference to it on the heap because storing it directly in a struct isn't possible due to an unknown type and potential size differences. All class references have the same size.

The pattern works as follows:

1. Define a private, internal base class that acts as an abstract interface.
2. Define a second private, generic class that inherits from the base class. This class holds the actual concrete `Logger`.
3. The public-facing `AnyLogger` struct contains an instance of the base abstract interface.

You can think of `AnyLogger` as a universal remote control. `AnyLogger` has a consistent set of buttons, in this case, the log method. The magic happens inside, where it can be programmed to control different types, like the `Logger`. The user doesn't need to understand the complex details of the remote internally.

Implementing a Type-Erased Wrapper

To build `AnyLogger<Message>` step-by-step, start by analyzing how each part contributes to the pattern.

Step 1: The Internal Blueprint

First, define the two private classes that will serve as the *box*. Classes are used because you need reference semantics to store them on the heap.

```
private class AnyLoggerBase<Message> {
  func log(_ message: Message) {
    fatalError("This method must be overridden")
  }
}

private class ConcreteLogger<Concrete: Logger>:
AnyLoggerBase<Concrete.Message> {
  private let implementation: Concrete

  init(_ implementation: Concrete) {
    self.implementation = implementation
  }

  override func log(_ message: Concrete.Message) {
    implementation.log(message)
  }
}
```

`AnyLoggerBase` is the base class that functions as the wrapper's "abstract interface." It is generic over `Message` to match the public struct's generic parameter. The `fatalError` in the base class indicates an "abstract" class — it's not meant to be used directly, only subclassed.

`ConcreteLogger` is the generic class that contains the concrete logger. It inherits from the base class and overrides its methods.

Step 2: The Public-Facing Wrapper

Now define the `AnyLogger` struct and expose it as an external API for consumption.

```
struct AnyLogger<Message>: Logger {
  private let base: AnyLoggerBase<Message>

  init<Concrete: Logger>(_ logger: Concrete) where
Concrete.Message == Message {
    self.base = ConcreteLogger(logger)
  }
```

```
    func log(_ message: Message) {
      base.log(message)
    }
  }
```

What really matters is the generic initializer. When you create an `AnyLogger`, you specify a concrete `Logger` instance, like a `FileLogger` or `ConsoleLogger` defined in Chapter 2. The initializer then creates a `ConcreteLogger` for that type and stores it in the base property. The `where Concrete.Message == Message` clause ensures that during compilation, you can't accidentally use a `Logger` that expects `Data` as an `AnyLogger<String>`.

Step 3: Using the Wrapper

With the `AnyLogger` wrapper in place, you can store different types of loggers, like `FileLogger` and `ConsoleLogger`, in a single, homogeneous collection. Instead of working directly with `any Logger` existential, you now have a concrete type, `AnyLogger<String>`, which offers a simple interface.

```
let fileLogger = FileLogger()
let consoleLogger = ConsoleLogger()

let stringLoggers: [AnyLogger] = [
  AnyLogger(fileLogger),
  AnyLogger(consoleLogger)
]

for logger in stringLoggers {
  logger.log("This message is sent to all loggers.")
}
```

This follows the same pattern Apple uses for APIs like `AnyPublisher` from Combine and `AnyView` from SwiftUI. While it offers maximum flexibility, it comes at the expense of performance due to heap allocation and dynamic dispatch. It should only be used when a generic approach is not feasible.

Anatomy of a Generic: Deconstructing Result

`Result` is one of the most commonly used generics in Swift. You often use it when writing networking services and processing responses. It's a perfect example of how generics can create elegant, expressive, and incredibly safe APIs. It's an amalgamation of the concepts you've learned so far, and by analyzing its design, you can see how well they work together to solve common programming problems, for example, handling the result of an operation that can either succeed or fail.

The Result Enum and Its Error Constraint

Before the introduction of `Result`, Swift developers usually relied on tuples for writing those methods. For example, while writing a networking service, tuples like `(Data?, Error?)` were often used. This approach was a major source of ambiguity, forcing developers to check all possible states. This led to a pyramid of doom with `if-let` chaining or deep nesting of `guard let`, resulting in code that was both frail and difficult to read.

The `Result` type solves this problem with the power and clarity of a generic type. At its core, `Result` is an enum with two mutually exclusive cases:

```
@frozen enum Result<Success, Failure: Error> {
  case success(Success)
  case failure(Failure)
}
```

This is a powerful concept that represents a value limited to one of several distinct options. As an enum, an instance of `Result` can only be in one of these states at a time, holding either a `.success` or a `.failure`, but never both. This straightforward structure eliminates the ambiguity present in the old tuple-based approach.

The `Failure` type in the `Result` generic is restricted to elements that conform to Swift's standard `Error` protocol. This ensures that `Result` integrates smoothly with Swift's error handling system. This standardization is extremely powerful, enabling you to write generic methods that can, for example, log the error from any `Result` type, confident that the failure will always be a descriptive `Error`.

Analyzing Generic Methods: map and flatMap

The true elegance of `Result` lies in its generic methods, which let you chain operations together in a clean, functional style. These important methods are `map` and `flatMap`.

map: Transforming a Successful Value

The `map<NewSuccess>` only transforms the `Result` when the result is a success. If the result is a failure, the `map` does nothing and simply passes the error along. Its simplified signature looks like this:

```
func map<NewSuccess>(_ transform: (Success) -> NewSuccess) ->
Result<NewSuccess, Failure>
```

It takes a closure with a `Success` and transforms it into a `NewSuccess`, then returns a new `Result` containing the value, while leaving the `Failure` unchanged. This is especially useful for processing data. For example, if you have a `Result<Data, Error>`, you can map it into a `Result<UIImage, Error>` without needing to manually check for a successful case first.

Here is a sample usage of the `map` function.

```
struct User: Decodable {
  let id: Int
  let name: String
  let username: String
}

enum FetchError: Error {
  case networkUnavailable
  case invalidData
}

func fetchUserData() -> Result<String, FetchError> {
  let jsonString = """
    {
    "id": 1,
    "name": "Michael Scott",
    "username": "michaelscott"
```

```
    }
    """
  return .success(jsonString)
}


let fetchResult = fetchUserData() // 1

let userResult: Result<User, FetchError> = fetchResult.map
{ jsonString in // 2
  let data = Data(jsonString.utf8)
  let decoder = JSONDecoder()
  let user = try! decoder.decode(User.self, from: data)
  return user
}

switch userResult { // 3
case let .success(user):
  print("Success! Created user: \(user.id)")
case let .failure(error):
  print("Failure. Reason: \(error)")
}
```

Following is a breakdown of the whole situation:

1. Returns a `Result<String, FetchError>`.
2. Use `map` to transform the successful `String` into a `User` object.
3. Depending on what `fetchUserData()` returns, either `.success` or `.failure`.

flatMap: Chaining Operations That Can Also Fail

It is slightly more complex than the `map` function. You can use it when your transformation logic involves another operation that might fail as well. That's when your closure also returns a `Result`. `flatMap` helps avoid nested results, such as `Result<Result<User, Error>, Error>`. Its simplified signature is:

```
func flatMap<NewSuccess>(_ transform: (Success) ->
Result<NewSuccess, Failure>) -> Result<NewSuccess, Failure>
```

The main difference here is that the `flatMap` closure returns a `Result`. This allows you to chain multiple failable operations together cleanly. In summary, use `map` for simple transformations and use `flatMap` to chain another failable operation.

Consider the following example:

```
enum ProfileError: Error {
  case userNotFound
```

```
  case networkFailed
}

func fetchUserID(from username: String) -> Result<Int,
ProfileError> {
  if username == "jimhalpert" {
    return .success(3)
  } else {
    return .failure(.userNotFound)
  }
}

func fetchUserProfile(for userID: Int) -> Result<User,
ProfileError> {
  if userID == 3 {
    return .success(User(id: 3, name: "Jim Halpert", username:
"jimhalpert"))
  } else {
    return .failure(.networkFailed)
  }
}
```

Now, if you attempt the following:

```
let userResult = fetchUserID(from: "alex")

let result: Result<Result<User, ProfileError>, ProfileError> =
userResult.map { id in
  return fetchUserProfile(for: id) // This returns a
Result<User, ProfileError>
}
```

This will leave you with a chain of `Result<Result<User, ProfileError>, ProfileError>`. To fix that, you use `flatMap`

```
let result: Result<User, ProfileError> = userResult.flatMap { id
in
  return fetchUserProfile(for: id)
}
```

This gives you a clean `Result<User, ProfileError>`.

Result in Practice: Type-Safe Error Handling

`Result` provides a clear, safe API for common, practical scenarios, such as asynchronous network requests. Using `Result` for the method makes the definition straightforward. Check the snippet below:

```
enum NetworkError: Error {
  case invalidURL
  case networkRequestFailed
  case decodingFailed
}

func fetchUser(id: Int) async -> Result<User, NetworkError> {
  guard let url = URL(string: "https://api.example.com/users/\
(id)") else {
    return .failure(.invalidURL)
  }

  do {
    let (data, _) = try await URLSession.shared.data(from: url)
    let user = try JSONDecoder().decode(User.self, from: data)
    return .success(user)

  } catch is DecodingError {
    return .failure(.decodingFailed)
  } catch {
    return .failure(.networkRequestFailed)
  }
}
```

The code that invokes the method is forced by the compiler to manage both success and failure states. A `switch` statement is the clearest way to handle the outcome.

```
let result = await fetchUser(id: 2)
switch result {
case let .success(user):
  // Update the UI with the user object
case let .failure(error):
  // Show an error message to the user
}
```

This pattern offers three main advantages: **explicitness** (you must acknowledge both outcomes), **clarity** (the code's purpose is clear), and **type safety** (the compiler knows the specific types of user and error).

Key Points

- Writing multiple, similar concrete protocols (such as `UserDataSource` and `ProductDataSource`) is a sign of code duplication. The first step to writing generic code is to recognize these repeating patterns.
- A single generic protocol with an `associatedtype` creates a unified, abstract blueprint that can solve an entire class of problems, making your architecture more scalable and maintainable.
- The primary benefit of generic protocols isn't just consolidating definitions; it's enabling the creation of reusable *consumer* functions (such as a single `displayItemCount` function) that can operate on any conforming type.
- Protocols are not limited to one `associatedtype`. You can define multiple associated types to model complex contracts, such as a generic `APIRequest` with both a `RequestBody` and a `Response`.
- You can enforce universal rules by constraining an `associatedtype` directly in its definition (e.g., `associatedtype Item: Identifiable & Equatable`), making the protocol itself stricter and more self-documenting.
- The `where` clause is a more flexible tool for applying local constraints to a single function or extension, keeping the base protocol simple and more widely applicable. A common use of a `where` clause is to ensure that the associated types of two different generic types are the same (e.g., `where Response.Item == Cache.Item`).
- This compile-time check prevents a whole class of logical errors by ensuring you only operate on matching types, such as comparing `Users` to `Users`, not `Products`.
- **Specialization** is the compile-time process where Swift creates separate, concrete, and highly optimized copies of a generic function for each specific type it is used with.
- **Specialization** enables **devirtualization**, a critical optimization that replaces slower dynamic dispatch (e.g., a Protocol Witness Table lookup) with direct, high-performance static dispatch.
- The main trade-off for the incredible runtime performance of generics is a potential increase in the final app's **binary size**.

- The best and most performant solution to the PAT problem is to use a generic constraint (e.g., `<T: Logger>`) instead of an existential, as this leverages specialization.
- Swift's `Result<Success, Failure: Error>` is a prime example of a generic enum that provides type-safe error handling by representing one of two mutually exclusive states.
- Use a `map` on a `Result` for simple, non-failable transformations of a success value. Use `flatMap` to chain an operation that can also fail, avoiding nested `Result` types.

Where to Go From Here?

Congratulations, you've reached the end of the chapter. In this chapter, you learned about the benefits and trade-offs of generics. You also found some answers to the questions you might have had from Chapter 2. Give yourself a pat on the back because you also wrote your own type erasure.

The goal of this chapter was not only to turn you into a *pro* with generics and familiarize you with its details but also to encourage you to consider all the trade-offs of writing abstract code, which will ultimately help you think like an experienced engineer.

Section II: Execution, Concurrency, & The Compiler

The chapters in this section focuses on what happens after code is written but before it runs. You'll follow Swift code through the compiler pipeline, including SIL generation, optimization passes, and machine code emission. It explains ARC, memory layout, and ownership rules, then shows when and how to safely step outside them using Unsafe Swift.

You'll also learn how to use compiler diagnostics and tools to identify performance bottlenecks and write code that is both fast and correct.

Chapter 4: Embracing Structured Concurrency

Aaqib Hussain

Ever since Apple introduced `async/await` and actors, writing concurrent code has changed fundamentally. Structured concurrency offers a level of simplicity and safety that was missing in older APIs such as `DispatchQueue` and `OperationQueue`. If writing asynchronous code with `DispatchQueue` was often a matter of "Somehow, I manage", then writing it with structured concurrency is confidently "Of course, I manage."

This modern system enables you to write thread-safe code that is less prone to race conditions from the start, as the compiler actively guides you away from potential issues.

This chapter examines Apple's entire async ecosystem. You will go beyond the basics to master Task hierarchies, ensure UI safety with the Main Actor, and process asynchronous data streams. Brace yourself, an adventure is coming...

Mastering Structured Concurrency

If you often write asynchronous code, you're likely aware of how it can create a chaotic web of completion blocks and disconnected queues. This makes it difficult to track the lifecycle of work items or to handle cancellations properly.

On the other hand, while `async/await` introduces clean syntax, its real power lies in the structure it provides. It not only enforces a formal hierarchy but also provides a clear and predictable order to that chaos. Additionally, it provides compile-time safety and a runtime system that automatically manages complex scenarios, such as parallel execution and cancellation, which helps prevent common bugs and resource leaks.

The Task Hierarchy: More Than Just a Closure

In Swift, a `Task` is not just a closure that runs on a background thread, but a container that concurrently runs work that the system actively manages. Each `Task` has a priority, can be cancelled, and exists within its own hierarchy, the **Task Tree**.

When an `async` method runs, it runs within a `Task`. If that method creates a new task, the outer task becomes the **parent** and the new task becomes the **child**. This can create a tree-like structure consisting of parents and children.

In Swift's structured concurrency, there are two main ways to create child tasks: `async let` (implicit) and `TaskGroup` (explicit). The key difference between them is their use case:

- Use `async let` when you know the exact number of concurrent operations you need.
- Use a `TaskGroup` when you need to create a varying number of concurrent tasks, often within a loop, which gives you more flexibility over the priority.

In both cases, the tasks created are child tasks. This means they automatically become part of their parent tasks' lifecycles. They are cancelled when their parent task is cancelled, and they will automatically escalate the parent's priority if created with a higher priority while the parent awaits their result.

Consider the following example of an implicit child:

```
struct UserProfile {
  var name: String
  var handle: String
}

struct ActivityItem {
  var description: String
}

func fetchProfile() async throws -> UserProfile {
  print("Child 1 (Profile): Fetching...")
  try await Task.sleep(for: .seconds(1)) // Simulate work
```

```
  print("Child 1 (Profile): Finished.")
  return UserProfile(name: "Michael Scott", handle:
"@michaelscott")
}

func fetchFeed() async throws -> [ActivityItem] {
  print("Child 2 (Feed): Starting loop...")
  for i in 0..<100 {
    // This sleep is a cancellation point
    try await Task.sleep(for: .milliseconds(500))
    // This line will not be printed after cancellation
    print("Child 2 (Feed): Completed iteration \(i)")
  }
  return []
}

func loadUserProfileAndActivityFeed() async {
  print("Parent: Starting to fetch data.")
  // 1
  async let profileTask = fetchProfile()
  async let feedTask = fetchFeed()

  do {
    let (profile, feed) = try await (profileTask, feedTask) // 2
    print("Parent: Successfully loaded profile for \(profile)
and \(feed.count) activity items.")
  } catch {
    print("Parent: One of the child's tasks was cancelled or
threw an error.")
  }
}
```

Here's a breakdown of everything above:

1. Creates two implicit children, i.e., `profileTask` and `feedTask`.
2. This code waits for both children to complete or for either to be cancelled. This waits asynchronously; depending on system resources, the operations may execute concurrently. That `fetchFeed()` does not necessarily wait for `fetchProfile()` to finish.

So if you were to do this:

```
let mainTask = Task {
  await loadUserProfileAndActivityFeed()
}
```

You'll see the following printed in the console:

```
Parent: Starting to fetch data.
```

```
Child 1 (Profile): Fetching...
Child 2 (Feed): Starting loop...
Parent: Starting to fetch data.
Child 1 (Profile): Fetching...
Child 2 (Feed): Starting loop...
Child 2 (Feed): Completed iteration 0
Child 2 (Feed): Completed iteration 1
Child 2 (Feed): Completed iteration 2
Child 1 (Profile): Finished.
Child 2 (Feed): Completed iteration 3
Child 2 (Feed): Completed iteration 4
Child 2 (Feed): Completed iteration 5
...
```

At any point during the execution of the loop, if you cancel the task, you can cancel it like:

```
mainTask.cancel()
```

The amazing thing about this is automatic propagating cancellation. If the parent task is cancelled, Swift sends a cancellation signal down to all its children and their subsequent children.

And your console would print:

```
Parent: One of the child's tasks was cancelled or threw an
error.
```

Now, at // 1. You could alternatively do this:

```
func loadUserProfileAndActivityFeed() async {
  print("Parent: Starting to fetch data.")

  do {
    let profileTask = try await fetchProfile() // 1
    let feedTask = try await fetchFeed() // 2

    let (profile, feed) = (profileTask, feedTask)
    print("Parent: Successfully loaded profile for \(profile)
and \(feed!.count) activity items.")
  } catch {
    print("Parent: One of the child's tasks was cancelled or
threw an error.")
  }
}
```

Although it still works asynchronously, this approach has a disadvantage.

Specifically:

1. `fetchProfile()` must finish before moving on.
2. `fetchFeed()` only starts after `fetchProfile()` completes.

> **Note**: Between these two approaches, i.e., `async-let` or awaiting each method directly, choose carefully based on your needs and the situation.

The `async-let` approach works well when you know the exact number of child tasks you need to execute. When dealing with a dynamic number of child tasks, the best choice is to use `TaskGroup`. A task group provides a scope that runs tasks in parallel and waits for all of them to finish before exiting.

To better understand this, you can revisit the original `loadUserProfileAndActivityFeed()` method and rewrite it using a task group. One constraint here is that this approach relies on a single return type, which you can handle cleanly with an enum, like this:

```
enum FetchResult {
  case profile(UserProfile)
  case feed([ActivityItem])
}

func loadUserProfileAndActivityFeed() async {
  print("Parent: Starting to fetch data.")

  do {
    // Create variables to hold the results from the group
    var profile: UserProfile?
    var feed: [ActivityItem]?

    try await withThrowingTaskGroup(of: FetchResult.self)
{ group in // 1
      // Add child tasks to the group. They run in parallel.
      group.addTask {
        return .profile(try await fetchProfile()) // 2
      }

      group.addTask {
        return .feed(try await fetchFeed()) // 3
      }

      // Collect the results as they complete
      for try await result in group { // 4
        switch result {
        case let .profile(fetchedProfile):
```

```
          profile = fetchedProfile
        case let .feed(fetchedFeed):
          feed = fetchedFeed
        }
      }
    }

    // The group has finished, and you can now use the results.
    print("Parent: Successfully loaded profile for \(profile)
and \(feed!.count) activity items.")
  } catch {
    print("Parent: One of the child's tasks was cancelled or
threw an error.")
  }
}
```

Here's a walkthrough of the logic in this snippet:

1. Creates a concurrent work scope and specifies the data type returned by each child task.
2. Tries to `fetchProfile()`.
3. Tries to `fetchFeed()`.
4. Iterates over the `group` and retrieves data from every task as it arrives asynchronously.

Understanding Task Priority

Every task you create has a priority, which indicates how important its work is to the system. The system uses this priority to decide which task to schedule on an available thread, especially when there are more tasks ready to run than CPU cores available.

Swift provides a variety of `TaskPriority` levels, from highest to lowest:

1. `.high`: For tasks that need to be completed "as soon as possible".
2. `.userInitiated`: Similar to `.high`, but semantically tied to work requested by the user and expected to be completed quickly.
3. `.medium`: The default priority when none is specified.
4. `.low`: For tasks that are not time-sensitive, but whose results the user might eventually see.

5. `.utility`: For long-running tasks that the user doesn't directly track, like background fetch operations.

6. `.background`: For cleanup, maintenance, or other work that can happen when the device is idle.

You can specify the priority of a task like this:

```
Task(priority: .background) {
  // Perform cleanup work here...
  print("Cleaning up old files on priority: \
(Task.currentPriority)")
}
```

A key feature of the system is priority escalation. If a low-priority parent task awaits a high-priority child task, the system temporarily escalates the parent's priority to match the child's. This helps prevent high-priority work from being blocked by low-priority work. This process is known as **priority inversion**, where high-priority work is indirectly blocked by lower-priority work.

Task Cancellation

Some asynchronous tasks might take longer than expected. For example, downloading a large image or a PDF could cause the user to cancel the process. In such cases, each task should check for cancellation. There are two ways to do this: using `Task.isCancelled` or by using `try Task.checkCancellation()`. Here's how you do it:

```
func fetchFeed() async throws -> [ActivityItem] {
  print("Child 2 (Feed): Starting loop...")
  for i in 0..<100 {
    // Cancellation check
    if Task.isCancelled {     //
      throw CancellationError()  // 1
    }       //

    // This sleep is a cancellation point
    try await Task.sleep(for: .milliseconds(500))

    // This line will not be printed after cancellation
    print("Child 2 (Feed): Completed iteration \(i)")
  }
  return []
}
```

So, what is happening here?

1. It checks whether the task is cancelled and throws a cancellation error if it is. To achieve similar results, you can replace this check with `try Task.checkCancellation()`.

While using a task group, you can also use `.addTaskUnlessCancelled` to add child tasks. It only adds a new child if the parent task is still running. You can modify the original method as follows:

```
func loadUserProfileAndActivityFeed() async {
  print("Parent: Starting to fetch data.")

  do {
    // ...

    try await withThrowingTaskGroup(of: FetchResult.self)
{ group in // 1
      // Add child tasks to the group. They run in parallel.
      group.addTask {
        return .profile(try await fetchProfile())
      }

      group.addTaskUnlessCancelled {
        return .feed(try await fetchFeed())
      }

      // ...
    }
  } catch {
    print("Parent: One of the child's tasks was cancelled or
threw an error.")
  }
}
```

Cooperative Cancellation with Task.yield()

In concurrent systems, it's important for long-running tasks to be considerate. A task that performs heavy CPU-based computation without taking any breaks can monopolize a thread, blocking other tasks from executing. To address this, Swift offers `Task.yield()`.

`Task.yield()` is an `async` function that briefly pauses the current task, enabling the system to schedule and run other pending tasks. This is a form of cooperative multitasking.

You should use `Task.yield()` inside long loops that don't contain other `await` calls. This ensures your tasks remain cooperative.

Without `yield()`, a long-running task is like a person at the gym who sits at the bench press, endlessly scrolling the internet while everyone waits for their turn. `Task.yield()` is you politely standing up between sets to let someone else work out.

Now, consider the case where you have two loops in two separate tasks: `taskA` and `taskB`

```
let taskA = Task {
  print("Task A: Starting a long loop.")
  for i in 0..<10 {
    print("Task A: Now on iteration \(i)")
  }
  print("Task A: Finished")
}

let taskB = Task {
  print("Task B: Starting a long loop.")
  for i in 0..<10 {
    print("Task B: Now on iteration \(i)")
  }
  print("Task B: Finished")
}
```

If you run the tasks, you'll see output similar to the following:

```
Task A: Starting a long loop.
Task A: Now on iteration 0
...
Task A: Finished
Task B: Starting a long loop.
Task B: Now on iteration 0
...
Task B: Finished
```

Now, if you want to use concurrent execution, `Task.yield()` comes into play as shown below:

```
let taskA = Task {
  print("Task A: Starting a long loop.")
  for i in 0..<5 {
    await Task.yield()
    print("Task A: Now on iteration \(i)")
  }
  print("Task A: Finished")
}

let taskB = Task {
  print("Task B: Starting a long loop.")
  for i in 0..<5 {
    await Task.yield()
```

```
    print("Task B: Now on iteration \(i)")
  }
  print("Task B: Finished")
}
```

By adding `await Task.yield()`, each task voluntarily pauses during each iteration, passing control back to the system scheduler. The scheduler then allows the other task to run, leading to interleaved execution as shown in the example below. Although the exact order can vary, the tasks will share execution time properly.

```
Task A: Starting a long loop.
Task B: Starting a long loop.
Task A: Now on iteration 0
Task B: Now on iteration 0
Task A: Now on iteration 1
Task B: Now on iteration 1
...
```

This cooperative behavior is essential to ensure that long-running tasks don't starve other parts of your program, keeping your app responsive.

Tasks: Breaking the Structure

Swift provides robustness and control through a parent-child hierarchy in structured concurrency, which you learned previously. In addition, Swift provides **Unstructured Concurrency**. Unlike tasks that are in a parent-child relationship, an unstructured task is independent and doesn't rely on a parent task. It provides complete flexibility to manage tasks however you need. It inherits the surrounding context; for example, if created in a `@MainActor` scope, it inherits that isolation. It also inherits priority and task-local values. You can use `@TaskLocal static var` to create a task-scoped value that is visible to child tasks.

```
struct RequestInfo {
  @TaskLocal static var requestID: UUID?
}

func handleTaskRequest() async {
  await RequestInfo.$requestID.withValue(UUID()) {
    if let id = RequestInfo.requestID {
      print("Processing order with ID: \(id)") // 1
    }

    // Create a child task
    let childTask = Task {
      // The child task "gets a copy" of the parent's task-local
values
```

```
      if let id = RequestInfo.requestID {
        print("Child task logging for ID: \(id)") // 2
      }
    }
    await childTask.value
  }
}
```

Consider if the UUID is `AE9FF928-5638-4877-A0F9-9D231C13D48B`, and you run the method `handleTaskRequest()`

1. Prints "Processing order with ID: AE9FF928-5638-4877-A0F9-9D231C13D48B"
2. Also prints "Child task logging for ID: AE9FF928-5638-4877-A0F9-9D231C13D48B"

Conversely, Swift offers a task that is entirely independent of the scope in which it's running. It doesn't inherit any priority or local task variables. Although you can specify a priority for the task, as with a normal `Task`, such a task is called a **detached task**. You create it by calling `Task.detached { ... }`.

Check the example below:

```
func handleDetachedRequest() async {
  await RequestInfo.$requestID.withValue(UUID()) {

    if let id = RequestInfo.requestID {
      print("Processing order with ID: \(id)") // 1
    }

    let detachedTask = Task.detached { // 2
      print("Detached Task: Starting...")

      if let id = RequestInfo.requestID { // 3
        print("Detached Task: Inherited request ID \(id)")
      } else {
        print("Detached Task: I have no request ID. I am
independent.")
      }
    }

    await detachedTask.value
  }
}
```

For simplicity, you can assume the UUID is the same as the previous one: `AE9FF928-5638-4877-A0F9-9D231C13D48B`. Then, running the method `handleDetachedRequest()` would produce the following output.

1. Prints "Processing order with ID: AE9FF928-5638-4877-A0F9-9D231C13D48B".
2. The `Task.detached {}` scope prints "Detached Task: Starting...".
3. The detached scope doesn't affect the parent scope. It prints "Detached Task: I have no request ID. I am independent."

Data Isolation

Because an app often handles many concurrent tasks, two (or more) tasks can try to update a shared state at the same time, leading to a data race. To prevent this, Swift enforces data isolation to ensure that your data is always correct when accessed and that no other thread modifies it concurrently. There are three ways to isolate data.

1. Since immutable data cannot be changed, it is always isolated. This prevents other code from modifying it while you access it.
2. A local variable inside a task is always isolated because no other code outside the task has a reference to it. Similarly, Swift ensures a closure is not used concurrently when it captures a variable.
3. Data within an actor is isolated, and its methods are the only safe way to access it. If multiple tasks try to call these methods simultaneously, the actor forces them to "wait their turn," ensuring only one can run at a time.

Advanced Actors and Data Safety

Actors are fundamental to modern Swift concurrency. They offer a robust, compiler-verified way to prevent data races. By isolating state and enforcing serialized access, they address many traditional issues in multithreaded programming. However, actors are not a perfect solution. They introduce their own challenges and complex behaviors that must be understood to maximize efficiency. Below, you'll learn some of the challenges and advanced techniques for controlling actor execution and understanding their place in the broader ecosystem of thread-safety patterns.

The Reentrancy Problem Explained

An actor's primary feature is to execute methods one at a time, preventing multiple threads from accessing its state simultaneously. However, there is an exception known as **Actor Reentrancy**.

Actor Reentrancy is a concurrency concept where a function pauses (for example, at an await) and, while waiting for its completion, another task can enter (or re-enter) the same actor and execute other code, potentially modifying the actor's shared state before the original function resumes.

The problem is making incorrect assumptions about an actor's state across an `await`. To illustrate this, consider the following, which is vulnerable to reentrancy.

```
actor ProgressTracker {
  var loadedValues: [String] = []

  func load(_ value: String) async {
    // 1
    let expectedCount = loadedValues.count + 1
    print("Starting load for '\(value)'. Expecting count to be \
(expectedCount).")

    loadedValues.append(value)

    // 2
    try? await Task.sleep(for: .seconds(1))

    // 4
    print("Finished load for '\(value)'. Expected \
(expectedCount), but actual count is now: \
(loadedValues.count)")
  }
}

let tracker = ProgressTracker()
Task { await tracker.load("A") }
Task { await tracker.load("B") } // 3
```

When you run this code, the output is unpredictable and often incorrect:

```
Starting load for 'A'. Expecting count to be 1.
Starting load for 'B'. Expecting count to be 2.
Finished load for 'A'. Expected 1, but actual count is now: 2
Finished load for 'B'. Expected 2, but actual count is now: 2
```

The log for task "A" is incorrect. This happens because:

1. Task A starts `load("A")`, sets `expectedCount` to 1, and appends "A".
2. Task A hits `await` and suspends, allowing the actor to process other work.
3. Task B starts `load("B")`, sees that `loadedValues` contains 1 item, sets `expectedCount` to 2, and appends "B".
4. Task A resumes and prints its final message, but `loadedValues.count` is now 2, which violates A's original expectation.

This interleaving doesn't cause a crash but leads to unusual and unexpected behavior if you assume that the state remains unchanged across an `await`.

Preventing Reentrancy

You can eliminate this problem using the following rules:

1. If possible, perform all critical state mutations before the initial `await` call within a method.
2. Never assume that the state you read before an `await` will remain the same after it resumes. If you need the latest state, re-read it from the actor's properties.
3. For complex operations that require reentrancy avoidance, traditional locking mechanisms may be necessary, even within an `actor`.

Customizing Execution with SerialExecutor

By default, an actor's code runs on a shared global concurrency thread pool managed by the Swift runtime. At any given time, the system determines the most efficient execution strategy. While this generally works well, in certain cases, you might want the actor's code to execute on a *particular* thread or a serial queue. This can be achieved with a **custom executor**.

A common example is performing UI updates safely on the main thread using the global actor attribute `@MainActor`, either on an `actor` directly or via a method. This approach is convenient; however, building a custom executor from scratch can help you understand how threads work within an `actor`. A use case for such an executor is interfacing with an older C library, writing files serially, or working with an API that isn't thread-safe and requires all interactions to occur on a single, specific `DispatchQueue`.

> **@MainActor** is a global actor that controls the execution context on the main thread. By annotating functions, classes, or actors, you isolate that code to run on the main thread. This enables the compiler to verify safety at compile time, a key advantage over the older `DispatchQueue.main`.

A serial executor requires implementing `func enqueue(_ job: UnownedJob)`.

```
final class BackgroundQueueExecutor: SerialExecutor {
  // A shared instance for all actors that might use it
  static let shared = BackgroundQueueExecutor()

  // The specific queue you want your actor's code to run on
  private let backgroundQueue = DispatchQueue(label:
"com.kodeco.background-executor", qos: .background)

  func enqueue(_ job: UnownedJob) { // 1
    backgroundQueue.async {
      job.runSynchronously(on: self.asUnownedSerialExecutor())
    }
  }
}
```

1. This is the heart of the executor. It executes the submitted job. It's called "synchronously" because `backgroundQueue.async` has already handled the asynchronous scheduling.

Now, you can create an actor that uses this executor. By overriding the `unownedExecutor` computed property inside the actor, you tell the Swift runtime that all work for this actor must be scheduled via the custom executor.

```
actor LegacyAPIBridge {
  private let _unownedExecutor: UnownedSerialExecutor
  init(unownedExecutor: UnownedSerialExecutor =
BackgroundQueueExecutor.shared.asUnownedSerialExecutor()) {
    _unownedExecutor = unownedExecutor
  }

  nonisolated var unownedExecutor: UnownedSerialExecutor {
    _unownedExecutor
  }

  func performUnsafeWork() {
    // Thanks to our custom executor, this code is now
guaranteed
    // to run on
`BackgroundQueueExecutor.shared.backgroundQueue`.
    print("Performing work on a specific queue...")
```

```
    }
}
```

Custom executors are an advanced feature that offer the ultimate control for integrating Swift actors with specific threading needs, ensuring safety and compatibility with older code.

Bridging Concurrency Realms

Swift Concurrency did not emerge in isolation. For years, Combine served as Apple's modern, declarative framework for managing asynchronous events. It brought a powerful functional approach to handling streams of values over time. As a result, many mature and reliable codebases have a significant investment in Combine publishers, subscribers, and operators.

A key part of mastering modern Swift is learning how to connect these two realms. You rarely have the time to restart an existing project from scratch. More often, you'll introduce `async/await` into your current app. The aim is to provide a practical guide to interoperability that ensures both systems work together smoothly. This includes learning how to use a Combine publisher as a modern `AsyncSequence` and, conversely, how to wrap an `async` function for use in an older Combine-based workflow. Lastly, you'll explore high-level strategies for deciding when to create a bridge and when to perform a full migration.

From Combine to AsyncSequence

The most common situation you might encounter is using an existing Combine publisher from a ViewModel or an API layer in new `async/await` code. Swift makes this process quite straightforward. Every publisher provided by Combine has a property called `values` that is inherently an `AsyncSequence`. Much like the standard `Sequence` protocol allows you to iterate over a collection with a `for...in` loop, the `AsyncSequence` protocol lets you iterate over the values emitted by the publisher with a `for await...in` loop.

This is perfect for managing streams of data. For example, if you have a `PassthroughSubject` that emits live updates, you can handle it like this:

```
import Combine

enum UserActionEvent: String {
  case loginButtonTapped
  case dismissButtonTapped
  case logoutButtonTapped
```

```
}

let subject = PassthroughSubject<UserActionEvent, Never>()

// This task will run indefinitely, waiting for new values from
the publisher.
let combineListenerTask = Task {
  print("Listener: Waiting for values from Combine...")
  for await value in subject.values {
    print("Listener: Received '\(value)' from the publisher.")
  }
  print("Listener: Finished.")
}

// In another part of your code, you can send values through the
subject.
try await Task.sleep(for: .seconds(1))
subject.send(.loginButtonTapped)
try await Task.sleep(for: .seconds(1))
subject.send(.dismissButtonTapped)
try await Task.sleep(for: .seconds(1))
subject.send(.logoutButtonTapped)
combineListenerTask.cancel()
```

The `for await...in` loop pauses execution until the subject publisher emits a new value. When a value is sent, the task resumes, prints the value, and then pauses again, waiting for the next one. This creates a smooth and efficient bridge, allowing your modern concurrent code to subscribe to and respond to any existing Combine stream.

From async/await to Combine

The reverse case is also possible, where you have the latest code written with `async/await`, and you need to provide compatibility with an older part of the code that is built with Combine and expects a publisher. The standard approach here is to wrap the `async` call in a `Future` publisher.

A `Future` is a special publisher that eventually emits a success (or a failure) and then finishes. This one-time event dispatch makes it a perfect bridge for an `async` function that returns a single result.

Now consider the following code snippet:

```
enum FetchError: Error { case networkError }

func fetchUserName(id: Int) async throws -> String {
  try await Task.sleep(for: .seconds(1))
  if id == 123 {
```

```
    return "Ray Wenderlich"
  } else {
    throw FetchError.networkError
  }
}
```

You can wrap this in a `Future` that correctly propagates either the success value or the failure:

```
func userNamePublisher(for id: Int) -> Future<String, Error> {
  return Future { promise in
    Task {
      do {
        let username = try await fetchUserName(id: id)
        promise(.success(username))
      } catch {
        promise(.failure(error))
      }
    }
  }
}
```

Usage is as follows:

```
var cancellable: Set<AnyCancellable> = []
userNamePublisher(for: 123)
  .sink(
    receiveCompletion: { completion in
      switch completion {
      case .finished:
        print("Finished successfully")
      case let .failure(error):
        print("Failed with error: \(error)")
      }
    },
    receiveValue: { username in
      print("Received username: \(username)")
    }
  ).store(in: &cancellable)
```

This prints "Received username: Ray Wenderlich" and "Finished successfully" because the input is 123. If you pass something else, the failure block is executed.

One unique aspect of the `Future` publisher is that it starts working as soon as it's created, not when a subscriber connects. To make its behavior more similar to a typical publisher (which only performs work upon subscription), you can wrap it in a `Deferred` publisher:

```
func userNamePublisher(for id: Int) -> AnyPublisher<String,
```

```
Error> {
  return Deferred {
    Future<String, Error> { promise in
      Task {
        do {
          let username = try await fetchUserName(id: id)
          promise(.success(username))
        } catch {
          promise(.failure(error))
        }
      }
    }
  }.eraseToAnyPublisher()
}
```

This pattern reliably ensures that your async operation runs only when a subscriber in your Combine chain actually needs it.

Strategic Migration: When to Bridge and When to Rewrite

With these bridging tools, you face a decision when working with a mixed codebase: should you continue bridging the two realms or rewrite older Combine code to `async/await`?

Bridging is a low-risk, practical approach that enables gradual adoption.

- **Pros:** It uses well-established, thoroughly tested code. It enables teams to learn the new system without hindering feature development. It's ideal for integrating `async/await` features into a stable, complex Combine core.
- **Cons:** It adds cognitive overhead, as developers have to be proficient in both techniques. The bridge code can sometimes be confusing, and you may not be able to fully utilize the full set of structured concurrency features throughout the code.

Rewriting aims for a modern, consistent codebase.

- **Pros:** It offers a unified concurrency model, making it easier to read and maintain. It provides full access to modern concurrency features, often resulting in simpler, more direct code. It's especially appropriate for new projects.
- **Cons:** It requires more effort and is a high-risk undertaking. Rewriting stable, complex logic can introduce new bugs and demand more time and thorough training for the entire team to understand the system's new capabilities.

A hybrid or bridged codebase isn't a sign of weakness; rather, it reflects a mature, evolving project. The best strategy is to use bridges to maintain consistent progress while focusing on smaller, self-contained features for rewriting as resources and time allow.

Best Practices & Testability

The `async/await` syntax makes writing concurrent code much easier. While the keywords eliminate the complexity of callback hell, they don't automatically ensure a solid architecture in your implementation. Writing production-quality concurrent code requires following best practices to keep it clean, maintainable, efficient, and performant.

Best Practice 1: Focused async/await Methods

An `async` method should have a single, clear purpose. It's often easy to write an async function that handles a long chain of unrelated tasks, which can make the code hard to read, debug, and test.

```
func setupDashboard() async {
    // 1
    guard let user = try? await APIClient.shared.fetchUser() else
{ return }

    // 2
    let friends = try? await APIClient.shared.fetchFriends(for:
user)

    // 3
    var userImages: [UIImage] = []
    if let photoURLs = try? await
APIClient.shared.fetchPhotoURLs(for: user) {
        for url in photoURLs {
            if let data = try? await
APIClient.shared.downloadImage(url: url) {
                // 4
                let processedImage = await processImage(data)
                userImages.append(processedImage)
            }
        }
    }
    // ... update UI with all this data ...
}
```

This function is doing too much:

1. Fetches the user.
2. Fetches their friends.
3. Fetches and processes images.
4. Processes the data by converting it into an image.

A better approach is to break it down into smaller, focused, and more reusable async functions.

```
func fetchUser() async throws -> User { /* ... */ }
func fetchFriends(for user: User) async throws -> [Friend] { /
* ... */ }
func fetchAllImages(for user: User) async -> [UIImage] { /* ...
*/ }

func setupDashboard() async {
  do {
    let user = try await fetchUser()
    // Run remaining fetches in parallel for performance
    async let friends = fetchFriends(for: user)
    async let images = fetchAllImages(for: user)

    let (userFriends, userImages) = try await (friends, images)
    // ... update UI ...
  } catch {
    // ... handle error ...
  }
}
```

This way, you're leveraging the full capabilities of structured concurrency. Once the `User` is fetched, friends and images are retrieved asynchronously and in parallel.

Best Practice 2: Re-read State After await

This is the most important rule for writing correct code inside an `actor`. As mentioned earlier, any `await` is a suspension point where the `actor` can be re-entered by another task, which may change its state. Never assume that the state you read before an `await` will stay the same after it resumes. If your logic depends on the most up-to-date state, you must re-read it from the actor's properties after the `await` finishes.

Best Practice 3: Be Deliberate with @MainActor

You can annotate entire classes or view models with `@MainActor` to address UI update issues. While sometimes effective, it can also cause performance problems by forcing non-UI tasks (like data processing or file I/O) onto the main thread, making your app less responsive and more likely to hang. Be precise and only isolate the specific properties or methods that genuinely need to interact with the UI.

Best Practice 4: Make Methods async to Control Execution

Perhaps the biggest challenge `async/await` introduces is testability. When a function is only called inside a `Task` within an object, it's hard to write tests for that function because you're left testing only the side effects it creates. You don't have control over the function at all, like when it gets called, exactly when it finishes, and so on. This makes the tests flaky most of the time. To clarify this further, consider a `UserProfileViewModel` that calls `fetchUserProfile()`.

```
struct UserProfile {
  // ...
}

protocol UserProfileRepository {
  func fetchUserProfile() async -> UserProfile
}

class UserProfileViewModel {
  private let repository: UserProfileRepository
  init(repository: UserProfileRepository) {
    self.repository = repository
  }

  func fetchUserProfile() {
    Task {
      let userProfile = await repository.fetchUserProfile()
      // ...
      // display the profile
    }
  }
}
```

This implementation works perfectly. It fetches the `UserProfile`, which you can display. If you write tests for it, they'll look something like this:

```
class UserProfileRepositoryMock: UserProfileRepository {
  var fetchUserProfileCallsCount = 0
  // ...
  func fetchUserProfile() async -> UserProfile {
    fetchUserProfileCallsCount += 1
```

```
    return UserProfile()
  }
}

func testFetchProfile() throws {
  let repository = UserProfileRepositoryMock()
  let viewModel = UserProfileViewModel(repository: repository)
  viewModel.fetchUserProfile()
  XCTAssertEqual(repository.fetchUserProfileCallsCount, 1)
}
```

This test might seem fine at first, but when you run it, it may sometimes pass and sometimes fail because you have no control over the task inside the function. To fix this issue, you'll modify the method in the original implementation.

```
func fetchUserProfile() async {
  let userProfile = await repository.fetchUserProfile()
  // ...
  // display the profile
}
```

Then you update the test as follows:

```
func testFetchProfile() async throws {
  let repository = UserProfileRepositoryMock()
  let viewModel = UserProfileViewModel(repository: repository)
  await viewModel.fetchUserProfile()
  XCTAssertEqual(repository.fetchUserProfileCallsCount, 1)
}
```

Now, no matter how many times you run this test, it won't fail because you now control the order of execution.

Key Points

- Swift's structured concurrency establishes a clear hierarchy for asynchronous tasks by using a Task Tree with parent-child links to avoid common bugs such as resource leaks.
- In a structured Task Tree, cancelling a parent task automatically sends a cancellation signal to all its children and their subsequent children, ensuring a clean and predictable shutdown.
- When you have a fixed number of asynchronous operations that can run simultaneously, use `async let` to create true child tasks. This approach is simpler and more straightforward than a `TaskGroup` for this particular case.
- When you need to generate a varying number of child tasks at runtime, often within a loop, a `TaskGroup` is the appropriate tool. It offers a scope to handle these dynamic tasks collectively.
- All tasks added to a single `TaskGroup` must produce the same type of result. The common approach to managing different result types is to wrap them in a single enum with associated values.
- To make tasks cancellable, you need to periodically check for the cancellation signal using either `try Task.checkCancellation()` or by using a cancellable async function like `Task.sleep(for:)`.
- Priority is a signal given to the system to help it schedule tasks. High-priority tasks are for immediate user-facing work, while low-priority tasks are for non-critical maintenance.
- If a low-priority parent task awaits a high-priority child, the parent's priority is temporarily boosted to match the child's, preventing the high-priority work from getting stuck.
- In long-running, CPU-intensive loops without any await calls, use `await Task.yield()` to voluntarily pause the task and give the system a chance to run other work, keeping your app responsive.
- `Task` vs. `Task.detached`: A standard `Task { … }` creates an unstructured task that inherits context, such as actor isolation and priority, but it is not part of the cancellation hierarchy. A `Task.detached { … }` is completely independent and inherits nothing.

- An actor safeguards its mutable state by ensuring that only one task accesses its data at a time. It queues concurrent calls to enforce mutual exclusion, ensuring serialized access.
- Any await inside an actor method is a suspension point where another task can "re-enter" the actor and modify its state. Never assume the state remains unchanged across an await.
- To use an existing Combine publisher in `async/await` code, access its `.values` property, which exposes it as an `AsyncSequence` that you can iterate with a `for await…in` loop.
- To use a modern async function in an older Combine-based workflow, wrap the call in a `Future` publisher that emits a single value or failure.
- Each `async` method should have a single, clear responsibility. Avoid creating large, monolithic `async` functions that perform many unrelated tasks.
- A function that initiates asynchronous work should be marked `async`. This allows your test code to await its completion, giving you control over execution order and preventing flaky tests caused by race conditions.

Where to Go From Here?

You're no longer just using `async/await`; you're equipped with the architectural mindset to build robust concurrent features. The real victory lies in applying these tools in practical scenarios. Consider how you can prevent actor reentrancy, develop systems free of data leaks, and leverage the power of Task Trees.

The critical thinking skills you've gained in this chapter are the most valuable tools you'll carry forward, enabling you to not only write concurrent code but to do it exceptionally well.

Chapter 5: Demystifying Swift Compiler Magic

Aaqib Hussain

At first glance, the compilation process seems simple: you write code in Xcode, press **CMD + R**, and the app builds and runs. But does the compiler understand your Swift code "as is"? The answer is no.

Before your code can run, the compiler goes through a complex process. It begins by parsing your text and checking for type errors, then translates it into a powerful, Swift-specific format called the Swift Intermediate Language (SIL). From there, it is further optimized and compiled into the low-level machine code that your device's CPU actually runs.

Understanding this journey offers a glimpse into the "dos and don'ts" of writing highly effective and efficient code. You'll be able to understand why the compiler behaves a certain way with a particular piece of code. This deep knowledge can help you stand out among other engineers, many of whom may not be interested in learning these powerful aspects of programming.

The Swift Compiler Architecture: A Bird's-Eye View

So, what exactly happens when you press **CMD + R**? Swift's compiler kicks into gear. What does it do? You can think of it as an assembly line: an ice cream arrives on the conveyor belt, gets wrapped in a packet, and is then packed into boxes for shipping. Inside the Swift compiler, it's somewhat similar. Each section takes an input and produces an output for the next part.

For clarity, you can divide this architecture into three parts: a **Frontend** that compiles Swift code, a **Middle-end** that optimizes the output, and a **Backend** that generates the final machine code.

The Frontend: Understanding Your Code

The frontend is responsible for converting human-readable code (`.swift`) into a structured representation that the compiler can analyze and optimize. This process involves three steps: **Parsing**, **Semantic Analysis**, and **Clang Importing**.

Parsing

The parser is responsible for creating an Abstract Syntax Tree (AST). It contains no semantic or type information. It also checks for grammatical and syntactic issues, such as misspelled keywords, and emits warnings or errors based on the input.

> **Abstract Syntax Tree (AST)**:It's a tree data structure that illustrates the abstract structure of a program. Each node represents a part of the code, such as an expression or statement. It omits unnecessary details, such as parentheses and formatting, and retains only the essential information that the compiler or other tools need to understand the code.

Clang Importer

The Clang Importer reads Clang modules (such as `<UIKit/UIKit.h>`) and translates their C or Objective-C APIs into equivalent Swift APIs. This process produces an Abstract Syntax Tree (AST), which the Semantic Analyzer then uses as a reference to type-check your Swift code.

Semantic Analysis

The Semantic Analyzer takes in the AST, performs type checking and inference, emits warnings or errors for semantic issues, and finally transforms it into a fully type-checked AST.

The Middle-End: Optimization in SIL

The middle-end is where the magic happens. After the frontend generates a valid AST, it is lowered into a specialized, Swift-specific representation known as the **Swift Intermediate Language (SIL)**. SIL has two main stages: Raw and Canonical.

Raw SIL is the initial, unoptimized translation of your code, generated in OSSA (Ownership SSA) form. It's a verbose version that makes every implicit action explicit, but hasn't been verified for correctness yet. Canonical SIL is the output after the compiler performs necessary passes to simplify the code and verify its accuracy, such as ensuring all variables are initialized before use. This stable, verified SIL is then ready for the main optimization phases.

> **Ownership Static Single Assignment [OSSA]**:OSSA is an augmented version of SSA that ensures and validates ownership invariants for SSA values within SIL functions.
>
> OSSA's ownership rules enable the compiler to run a static check on its own intermediate code. This check, run during compilation, ensures that the code is free of memory leaks and use-after-free errors, thereby identifying bugs in the compiler's own code generation (SILGen) and optimization phases.
>
> SILGen generates OSSA and remains maintained through essential optimizations. During the SIL pipeline, it is eventually lowered to plain SSA, after which ownership validation cannot be performed.

SIL is the compiler's secret weapon: a high-level intermediate language fully aware of Swift's unique features, such as value types, enums, and protocols. This is essential because it allows the compiler to perform powerful, language-specific optimizations, such as **Automatic Reference Counting (ARC)**, **devirtualization**, and **generic specialization**, that would be impossible at a lower level.

So, how does the compiler accomplish all of this? It follows a series of steps, starting with **SIL generation** to create the initial *raw* SIL, then applying **SIL guaranteed transformations** to ensure correctness through dataflow diagnostics (such as detecting uninitialized variables), and finally executing **SIL optimizations** to perform additional high-level, Swift-specific enhancements, including Automatic Reference Counting optimizations, devirtualization, and generic specialization.

The Backend: Generating Machine Code with LLVM

The final stage of the process is powered by LLVM (Low Level Virtual Machine). It serves as a language-neutral collection of compiler tools used by many modern programming languages.

This optimized SIL is then lowered to LLVM IR (Intermediate Representation), a format no longer specific to Swift. LLVM excels at low-level, hardware-specific optimization. It takes LLVM IR, further optimizes it, and produces machine code that runs on your device's specific CPU architecture, such as ARM64 for iPhones or x86_64 for Intel-based Macs.

To illustrate how these pieces fit together, here is the complete pipeline:

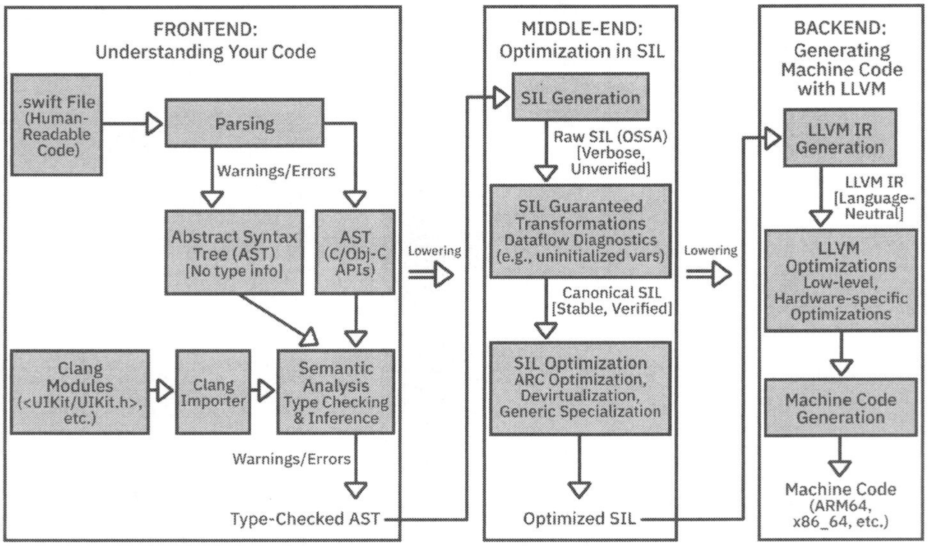

The Swift Compilation Pipeline

A Deep Dive into SIL

Having a complete overview of the compiler's process is important, but the most crucial part of this journey is the middle-end: SIL. Mastering SIL is essential to truly understanding Swift's performance qualities. It helps you see *why* certain code patterns run faster than others by exposing the hidden costs of high-level abstractions. Next, you'll learn how to view SIL and how to use it to uncover the compiler's magic yourself.

Why Does SIL Exist?

SIL is a specialized language used only within the Swift compiler. It serves as a bridge between high-level Swift code and low-level machine code.

To understand why SIL is necessary, consider the two representations at each end of the compiler pipeline:

- The AST is too high-level. It accurately represents the structure and intent of your code, but is too abstract for detailed performance analysis. It doesn't explicitly detail aspects like memory management or method dispatch.
- LLVM IR is too low-level. It is designed to be closer to hardware. By the time your code is converted to LLVM IR, it has already lost all knowledge of Swift-specific concepts, such as protocols, generics, and the distinction between structs and classes.

SIL exists in the optimal middle ground between these two worlds. It explicitly represents Swift's features, including each memory access, reference count, and protocol method call. This makes it an ideal language for the compiler to perform powerful optimizations before passing the code to LLVM. SIL is where the compiler reasons about your Swift code, allowing it to make intelligent decisions that uphold the language's safety and performance promises.

Generating and Reading SIL

You don't have to be a compiler engineer to understand SIL. You can even generate it yourself from any `.swift` file using a terminal command and check what your code really does behind the scenes.

You can generate the SIL using the Swift compiler on the command line. The most common command is:

```
swiftc -emit-sil -Onone Main.swift > Main.txt
```

This command will generate an unoptimized or canonical SIL and write it to `Main.txt`. This generates something similar to a debug version of the SIL. This is the final draft of canonical SIL before high-level optimizations.

You can also look at the pre-unoptimized SIL using `-emit-silgen`, which gives you the raw SIL. For performance analysis, the optimized version is preferred and can be generated with `-emit-sil -O`. By contrast, `-emit-sil -Onone` produces an unoptimized, debug-style SIL that's easier to read and reason about. It passes all the mandatory passes (like diagnostics) to ensure validity and skips the performance optimization passes, but doesn't reflect all the optimizations applied in a release build.

SIL has a syntax that looks like a low-level, verbose version of Swift. Consider the following function:

```
import Foundation

func add(_ a: Int, _ b: Int) -> Int {
  return a + b
}
```

Save it in a `Main.swift` file and execute the command stated above.

> **Warning**: SIL is not pretty. It looks like Swift code that has had way too much caffeine and feels the need to explain every step it takes. It makes every implicit action explicit, which is great for the computer but a headache for humans.

You should be able to see something like the following:

> **Note**: The Swift version used to generate these SIL listings is 6.0.3

```
sil_stage canonical

import Builtin
import Swift
import SwiftShims

import Foundation

func add(_ a: Int, _ b: Int) -> Int

// main // 1
sil @main : $@convention(c) (Int32,
UnsafeMutablePointer<Optional<UnsafeMutablePointer<Int8>>>) ->
Int32 {
bb0(%0 : $Int32, %1 :
```

```
$UnsafeMutablePointer<Optional<UnsafeMutablePointer<Int8>>>):
  %2 = integer_literal $Builtin.Int32, 0          // user: %3
  %3 = struct $Int32 (%2 : $Builtin.Int32)        // user: %4
  return %3 : $Int32                              // id: %4
} // end sil function 'main'

// add(_:_:)
sil hidden @$s4Main3addyS2i_SitF : $@convention(thin) (Int, Int)
-> Int { // 2
// %0 "a"                                         // users: %4,
%2
// %1 "b"                                         // users: %5,
%3
bb0(%0 : $Int, %1 : $Int):
  debug_value %0 : $Int, let, name "a", argno 1   // id: %2
  debug_value %1 : $Int, let, name "b", argno 2   // id: %3
  %4 = struct_extract %0 : $Int, #Int._value      // user: %7 //
3
  %5 = struct_extract %1 : $Int, #Int._value      // user: %7 //
  %6 = integer_literal $Builtin.Int1, -1          // user: %7 //
4
  %7 = builtin "sadd_with_overflow_Int64"(%4 : $Builtin.Int64,
%5 : $Builtin.Int64, %6 : $Builtin.Int1) : $(Builtin.Int64,
Builtin.Int1) // users: %9, %8 // 5
  %8 = tuple_extract %7 : $(Builtin.Int64, Builtin.Int1), 0 //
user: %11 // 6
  %9 = tuple_extract %7 : $(Builtin.Int64, Builtin.Int1), 1 //
user: %10 // 7
  cond_fail %9 : $Builtin.Int1, "arithmetic overflow" // id: %10
// 8
  %11 = struct $Int (%8 : $Builtin.Int64)         // user:
%12 // 9
  return %11 : $Int                               // id: %12
} // end sil function '$s4Main3addyS2i_SitF'

// static Int.+ infix(_:_:) // 10
sil public_external [transparent] @$sSi1poiyS2i_SitFZ :
$@convention(method) (Int, Int, @thin Int.Type) -> Int {
// %0                                             // user: %3
// %1                                             // user: %4
bb0(%0 : $Int, %1 : $Int, %2 : $@thin Int.Type):
  %3 = struct_extract %0 : $Int, #Int._value      // user: %6
  %4 = struct_extract %1 : $Int, #Int._value      // user: %6
  %5 = integer_literal $Builtin.Int1, -1          // user: %6
  %6 = builtin "sadd_with_overflow_Int64"(%3 : $Builtin.Int64,
%4 : $Builtin.Int64, %5 : $Builtin.Int1) : $(Builtin.Int64,
Builtin.Int1) // users: %8, %7
  %7 = tuple_extract %6 : $(Builtin.Int64, Builtin.Int1), 0 //
user: %10
  %8 = tuple_extract %6 : $(Builtin.Int64, Builtin.Int1), 1 //
user: %9
  cond_fail %8 : $Builtin.Int1, "arithmetic overflow" // id: %9
  %10 = struct $Int (%7 : $Builtin.Int64)         // user: %11
```

```
  return %10 : $Int                                // id: %11
} // end sil function '$sSi1poiyS2i_SitFZ'
```

The following outlines what is happening in the code:

1. Auto-generated by the compiler. The signature suggests two things: the function name is `main`, and it uses the C calling convention. This is essential so that the operating system knows how to call and run your program.
2. This is the function's full, mangled name. It's a unique identifier the compiler generates that encodes `Main.swift`, the function name (add), and the type signature.
3. These lines "unbox" the `Int` structs passed to the function (`%0` and `%1`) to extract the raw, machine-level 64-bit integer values (`_value`) from them.
4. `%6 = ... -1`: This creates the boolean flag `true` and stores it in register `%6`.
5. `%7 = ... (%4, %5, %6)`: This is the "safe add" instruction. The third parameter it takes (`%6`) is a flag that tells the function whether it should trap (crash the program) if the addition overflows.
6. The compiler first extracts the sum stored in `%8`.
7. Then the compiler extracts the overflow flag `%9` from the tuple returned by the addition.
8. The `cond_fail` instruction then checks this flag. If the flag is true, the program immediately traps (crashes) and reports an "arithmetic overflow." This is the explicit SIL implementation of Swift's default integer safety.
9. If the overflow check passes, the code extracts the sum `%8`, repacks it into a new Int struct, and finally returns it.
10. This block of SIL is the Swift Standard Library's actual implementation of the + operator for the Int type. The most important thing to notice is that the code inside is almost identical to the SIL generated for your own add function.

Tracing Performance with SIL

Reading SIL isn't just an exercise. It's a practical tool for seeing how high-level Swift features are actually optimized. It gives you definitive proof of performance characteristics.

Use Case 1: Witnessing Devirtualization

In Chapter 4, you learned that the compiler can replace indirect protocol calls with direct function calls through a process called devirtualization. With SIL, you can get concrete, visual proof of this optimization. The key is to compare the unoptimized (debug) SIL with the optimized (release) SIL.

The Before: Unoptimized SIL

First, look at the unoptimized SIL for our generic printThing function. When you compile without the `-O` flag, the compiler generates a generic "blueprint" of the function. Consider the following and generate the SIL for this:

```
protocol Printable { func printName() }
struct MyDevice: Printable { func printName()
{ print("Device") } }

func printThing<T: Printable>(_ thing: T) {
  thing.printName()
}
```

Inside the generic SIL function for `printThing<T>`, you will see this key instruction:

```
// ... inside the generic printThing<T> function ...
%2 = witness_method $T, #Printable.printName : ...
%3 = apply %2<T>(%0) : ...
```

The `witness_method` instruction is the smoking gun for dynamic dispatch. It's the SIL equivalent of telling the runtime, "I don't know the concrete type of T, so look up the correct printName implementation in the Protocol Witness Table."

The After: Optimized SIL

Now, when you compile with the `-O` flag (`swiftc -emit-sil -O ...`), the optimizer sees the specific call `printThing(MyDevice())`. It knows the concrete type is `MyDevice` and performs devirtualization and inlining. Inside this specialized context, the compiler no longer needs to guess. As you discovered, it often goes beyond just replacing `witness_method` with a direct `function_ref`. For small functions, it performs inlining by completely eliminating the function call and pastes the body of `MyDevice.printName()` directly into the call site. You can see this happening under the `sil @main` between `%45` to `%47`.

If the register numbers differ in your case, you should still be able to see the following under the `sil @main`.

```
  %45 = struct $String (%44 : $_StringGuts)       // user: %47
  // function_ref print(_:separator:terminator:)
  %46 = function_ref @$ss5print_9separator10terminatoryypd_S2StF
: $@convention(thin) (@guaranteed Array<Any>, @guaranteed
String, @guaranteed String) -> () // user: %47
  %47 = apply %46(%33, %40, %45) : $@convention(thin)
(@guaranteed Array<Any>, @guaranteed String, @guaranteed String)
-> ()
```

This is why `main` becomes so large in optimized SIL. It generates all the low-level SIL instructions to create the string "Device" and call the `print()` function. The calls to `printThing()` and `printName()` are removed entirely, eliminating the function-call overhead. This is devirtualization in its most aggressive and efficient form.

Use Case 2: Understanding ARC Overhead

Although ARC is a powerful feature, it comes with a performance cost. Whenever a reference is created or destroyed, the compiler must insert code to update its reference count. SIL makes this invisible cost visible.

Consider this simple class:

```
class Person {
  var name = "Michael Scott"
}

func greet(_ person: Person) {
  print("Hello, \(person.name)")
}

func createAndGreet() {
  let dwight = Person()
  greet(dwight)
```

```
}
```

Now generate the raw SIL and deconstruct `createAndGreet()` to see ARC overhead in action via OSSA.

```
// createAndGreet()
sil hidden [ossa] @$s4Main14createAndGreetyyF : ... {
bb0:
  // 1
  %2 = apply %1(%0) : ... -> @owned Person
  %3 = move_value %2 : $Person

  // 2
  %5 = begin_borrow %3 : $Person
  %7 = apply %6(%5) : ... (@guaranteed Person) -> ()
  end_borrow %5 : $Person

  // 3
  destroy_value %3 : $Person
  // ...
}
```

Below is the breakdown of the code stated above:

1. The `apply` instruction that creates the `Person` instance returns an `@owned Person`. The `@owned` keyword is explicit: it tells the compiler that this part of the code now "owns" the object and is responsible for releasing it, thereby increasing its reference count by +1. The `move_value` then transfers this ownership to the `dwight` constant.

2. This is the most interesting part. Instead of a `strong_retain` / `strong_release` pair around the call to greet, the compiler uses a more efficient `begin_borrow` / `end_borrow` pair. This is an optimization. The `greet` function takes its parameter as `@guaranteed`, meaning it promises not to destroy the object. The compiler uses this promise to safely "borrow" the reference for the duration of the call without needing to modify the reference count at all.

3. When the `dwight` constant goes out of scope at the end of the function, the `destroy_value` instruction is called. This is the OSSA equivalent of `strong_release`. It ends the lifetime of the owned reference, decrements the reference count, and will deallocate the object if the count reaches zero.

By examining the OSSA SIL, you can trace the exact lifecycle of your class instances and see how the compiler manages memory behind the scenes.

Becoming a Power User: Diagnostics and Flags

Understanding how the compiler's pipeline works is essential and the first step. The next step is learning how to interact with it like a power user. Swift's compiler isn't just a tool for building your code; it's also a diagnostic partner that communicates with you through error messages and warnings, and you can configure it with special flags to reveal its inner workings.

Here, you'll become familiar with how to interpret the compiler's language. You'll analyze a typical and complex generic error message to understand what the type checker is really telling you. Then, you'll investigate some key compiler flags that let you examine the compilation process, identify slow build times, and develop a deeper understanding of your code's performance.

Deconstructing Compiler Errors

Mostly, the rich and helpful errors (sometimes not so) that you see in Xcode come from the Semantic Analysis phase of the compiler. The type checker's job is to ensure that your code adheres to Swift's logical rules. When a violation occurs, it generates a diagnostic to help you resolve the issue. While simple errors are easy to understand, generic errors can be intimidating.

You can better understand these issues by deconstructing one of the most common generic errors: "Generic parameter 'T' could not be inferred."

Consider this simple generic function:

```
func createEmptyCollection<T: RangeReplaceableCollection>() -> T
{
  return T()
}
```

This function can create any kind of empty collection, like an Array or a String. But what happens when you call it like this?

```
// Error: Generic parameter 'T' could not be inferred.
let myThings = createEmptyCollection()
```

The code fails to compile. Here's the breakdown of the error message:

1. "Generic parameter `T`...": The compiler is helpfully pointing to the exact placeholder type it's struggling with.

2. "...could not be inferred.": "Inferred" means to figure something out from the surrounding context. The compiler is telling you, "You've asked me to create a collection of type `T`, but you haven't given me any clues as to what `T` should be. Should it be an `[Int]`? A `String`? I can't guess."

The function call provides no information about what `T` should be, and there's no other context to help. To fix this, you must provide the missing information with an explicit type annotation:

```
// The Fix: Provide an explicit type
let myThings: [Double] = createEmptyCollection()
```

Now the compiler has the clue it needs. It infers that `T` must be `[Double]` and the code compiles successfully. When you see "could not be inferred," your first thought should always be, "Where can I add a type annotation to give the compiler more context?"

Essential Compiler Flags

The `swiftc` command-line tool comes with several flags that can alter its behavior and produce different diagnostic information. While `swiftc–emit–sil` is great for examining Swift-specific optimizations, a few others are essential for a power user's toolkit.

```
-emit-ir
```

This flag instructs the compiler to halt after the LLVM IR generation phase and display the LLVM Intermediate Representation in the console.

```
swiftc -emit-ir Main.swift > Main.txt
```

LLVM IR is the final human-readable stage before machine code. It is much lower-level than SIL and is not specific to Swift. It resembles a complex, platform-agnostic assembly language. This helps you view the outcome of low-level optimizations and understand how your Swift code appears just before it becomes executable instructions.

A sample of the IR looks something like this.

```
; ModuleID = '<swift-imported-modules>'
source_filename = "<swift-imported-modules>"
target datalayout = "e-m:o-i64:64-i128:128-n32:64-S128"
target triple = "arm64-apple-macosx15.0.0"

@"\01l_entry_point" = private constant { i32, i32 } { i32 trunc
```

```
(i64 sub (i64 ptrtoint (ptr @main to i64), i64 ptrtoint (ptr
@"\01l_entry_point" to i64)) to i32), i32 0 }, section "__TEXT,
__swift5_entry, regular, no_dead_strip", align 4
@__swift_reflection_version = linkonce_odr hidden constant i16 3
@llvm.used = appending global [4 x ptr] [ptr @main, ptr
@"$s4Main3addyS2i_SitF", ptr @"\01l_entry_point", ptr
@__swift_reflection_version], section "llvm.metadata"

define i32 @main(i32 %0, ptr %1) #0 {
entry:
  ret i32 0
}

define hidden swiftcc i64 @"$s4Main3addyS2i_SitF"(i64 %0, i64
%1) #0 {
entry:
  %a.debug = alloca i64, align 8
  call void @llvm.memset.p0.i64(ptr align 8 %a.debug, i8 0, i64
8, i1 false)
  %b.debug = alloca i64, align 8
  call void @llvm.memset.p0.i64(ptr align 8 %b.debug, i8 0, i64
8, i1 false)
  store i64 %0, ptr %a.debug, align 8
  store i64 %1, ptr %b.debug, align 8
  %2 = call { i64, i1 } @llvm.sadd.with.overflow.i64(i64 %0, i64
%1)
  %3 = extractvalue { i64, i1 } %2, 0
  %4 = extractvalue { i64, i1 } %2, 1
  %5 = call i1 @llvm.expect.i1(i1 %4, i1 false)
  br i1 %5, label %7, label %6

6:                                                ; preds =
%entry
  ret i64 %3

7:                                                ; preds =
%entry
  call void @llvm.trap()
  unreachable
}

; Function Attrs: nocallback nofree nounwind willreturn
memory(argmem: write)
declare void @llvm.memset.p0.i64(ptr nocapture writeonly, i8,
i64, i1 immarg) #1

; Function Attrs: nocallback nofree nosync nounwind speculatable
willreturn memory(none)
declare { i64, i1 } @llvm.sadd.with.overflow.i64(i64, i64) #2

; Function Attrs: nocallback nofree nosync nounwind willreturn
memory(none)
declare i1 @llvm.expect.i1(i1, i1) #3
```

```
; Function Attrs: cold noreturn nounwind
declare void @llvm.trap() #4

attributes #0 = { "frame-pointer"="non-leaf" "no-trapping-
math"="true" "probe-stack"="__chkstk_darwin" "stack-protector-
buffer-size"="8" "target-cpu"="apple-a12" "target-
features"="+aes,+crc,+fp-armv8,+fullfp16,+lse,+neon,+ras,+rcpc,
+rdm,+sha2,+v8.1a,+v8.2a,+v8.3a,+v8a,+zcm,+zcz" }
attributes #1 = { nocallback nofree nounwind willreturn
memory(argmem: write) }
attributes #2 = { nocallback nofree nosync nounwind speculatable
willreturn memory(none) }
attributes #3 = { nocallback nofree nosync nounwind willreturn
memory(none) }
attributes #4 = { cold noreturn nounwind }

!llvm.module.flags = !{!0, !1, !2, !3, !4, !5, !6, !7, !8, !9, !
10, !11}
!swift.module.flags = !{!12}
!llvm.linker.options = !{!13, !14, !15, !16, !17}

!0 = !{i32 2, !"SDK Version", [2 x i32] [i32 15, i32 2]}
!1 = !{i32 1, !"Objective-C Version", i32 2}
!2 = !{i32 1, !"Objective-C Image Info Version", i32 0}
!3 = !{i32 1, !"Objective-C Image Info
Section", !"__DATA,__objc_imageinfo,regular,no_dead_strip"}
!4 = !{i32 4, !"Objective-C Garbage Collection", i32 100665088}
!5 = !{i32 1, !"Objective-C Class Properties", i32 64}
!6 = !{i32 1, !"Objective-C Enforce ClassRO Pointer Signing", i8
0}
!7 = !{i32 1, !"wchar_size", i32 4}
!8 = !{i32 8, !"PIC Level", i32 2}
!9 = !{i32 7, !"uwtable", i32 1}
!10 = !{i32 7, !"frame-pointer", i32 1}
!11 = !{i32 1, !"Swift Version", i32 7}
!12 = !{!"standard-library", i1 false}
!13 = !{!"-lswiftSwiftOnoneSupport"}
!14 = !{!"-lswiftCore"}
!15 = !{!"-lswift_Concurrency"}
!16 = !{!"-lswift_StringProcessing"}
!17 = !{!"-lobjc"}
```

This is generated for the add function that was discussed earlier.

Another practical diagnostic tool instructs the Swift frontend to measure how long it takes to type-check each function in your file.

```
swiftc -Xfrontend -debug-time-function-bodies Main.swift
```

This is an essential tool for diagnosing slow compile times. If your project takes a long time to build, this flag generates a list of your functions sorted by how many milliseconds the compiler spends on each. It quickly highlights the specific functions causing the delay during compilation, often those with complex expressions or poor type information that force the compiler to do extra work.

Summary of Useful Flags

Here is a quick reference table of the key flags discussed so far.

Flag	Purpose
`-emit-silgen`	Generates "raw" **SIL** (Swift Intermediate Language) — unoptimized, pre-diagnostic form of the Swift code.
`-emit-sil -Onone`	Generates canonical **SIL** (unoptimized) — typically used for debug builds.
`-emit-sil -O`	Generates canonical **SIL** (optimized) — used for release builds.
`-emit-ir`	Generates **LLVM IR** (Low-Level Intermediate Representation), showing the low-level code representation before machine code generation.
`-Xfrontend -debug-time-function-bodies`	Measures and logs compile time for each function, useful for identifying slow-compiling code.

Swift Compiler Inspection Flags

Attribute Magic: Guiding the Optimizer

Generally, Swift's compiler does an excellent job of optimizing. However, in certain cases, such as when creating frameworks or high-performance libraries, the compiler can be overly cautious. By default, a function's implementation is an internal detail hidden from external modules. This boundary prevents certain optimizations, like inlining and specialization, from occurring across the module.

This is where special attributes come into play. You can add these to your code to give the compiler direct instructions, granting it the permission and guidance it needs to perform those optimizations. Mastering them is a true "power user" skill that lets you tune the compiler to boost the performance of your public APIs.

@inlinable: Cross-Module Optimization

Normally, when you compile a library or framework, only the public API declarations are exposed to external modules, and the code itself remains opaque. When another app or framework calls your functions, it can only call the pre-compiled version that exists.

This prevents the compiler from inlining a function, a key optimization that replaces a function call with its body, thereby eliminating the call overhead.

In such cases, `@inlinable` is useful. By marking public functions with this attribute, you direct the compiler to include the function's source code (or equivalent form) in the module's interface.

Consider the following code residing in your library:

```
// In ScoreLibrary.swift
@inlinable
public func isScoreHigh(_ score: Int) -> Bool {
  return score > 100
}
```

And in your code, when using the library:

```
import ScoreLibrary

if isScoreHigh(250) { // <-- This call can be inlined
    // ...
}
```

Since the `isScoreHigh(_ score:Int)` function is inlinable, the compiler can see its body during compilation: `score > 100`. This allows it to replace the call with the comparison `250 > 100`, resulting in faster code execution.

The trade-off is that `@inlinable` reveals your implementation details and makes that specific code part of the public binary API.

@_specialize: Forcing Generic Specialization

As discussed in Chapter 3, generics perform specialization. This often stops happening across module boundaries. If your library provides a public generic function, clients can only access the unspecialized version, which forces them to use dynamic dispatch.

The @_specialize attribute is a powerful, though unofficial (hence the underscore), hint to the compiler. It directs the compiler: "When you compile this library, please create and export a pre-specialized, non-generic version of this function for the specific types I'm listing."

Imagine you have a function processValue<T>(_ value: T) in your library that you want to specialize and expose externally. You would do:

```
// In a library module
@_specialize(exported: true, where T == Int)
@_specialize(exported: true, where T == String)
public func processValue<T>(_ value: T) {
  print("Processing \(value)")
}
```

When this code compiles, it automatically includes three versions of the function: the main generic one, a specialized version for Int, and another for String. When an app imports this library and calls processValue(100), the linker can connect it directly to the fast, pre-compiled Int version, avoiding the overhead of dynamic dispatch. This may slightly increase binary size due to extra stored functions.

A Practical Use Case: Building a High-Performance Library

Now you can combine what you've learned so far to build a high-performance, generic utility function in a library.

Consider the following code:

```
// In Utilities.swift (Library Module)

// By combining @inlinable and @_specialize, you give the
compiler
// maximum opportunity to optimize.

@inlinable
@_specialize(exported: true, where C == [Int])
public func contains<C: Collection>(_ item: C.Element, in
collection: C) -> Bool where C.Element: Equatable {
  return collection.contains(item)
}
```

When this function is used from another module:

- If called with [Int]: The app can link directly to the fast, pre-specialized version of contains for an Array of Ints, thanks to @_specialize.

- If called with another type, like `Set<String>`, the app's compiler can "see" the body of the `contains` function because of `@inlinable` and can generate a freshly specialized and inlined version for `Set<String>` on the spot.

Using these attributes provides the compiler with all the information it needs to eliminate dynamic dispatch and produce the fastest code possible for your library's users.

Key Points

- Transforming your Swift code into a functioning app isn't a single step but a pipeline consisting of a **Frontend** (interpreting Swift code), a **Middle-end** (applying Swift-specific optimizations), and a **Backend** (producing machine code).
- The compiler's first step is to parse your code into an Abstract Syntax Tree (AST). This tree is a structured, hierarchical view of your code's logic, created after checking for basic syntax errors.
- A key part of the frontend, the Clang Importer, functions as a bridge. It reads C and Objective-C header files and converts their APIs into Swift-compatible ASTs, enabling smooth use of frameworks like UIKit and Foundation.
- The Semantic Analyzer is the frontend's "logic checker." It processes the ASTs from the parser and Clang Importer, performs type checking and inference, and outputs a fully validated, type-checked AST.
- The type-checked AST is transformed into Swift Intermediate Language (SIL). It's detailed enough for advanced optimization but still high-level enough to grasp Swift-specific concepts like protocols and value types.
- SIL has two main stages. **Raw** SIL is the initial, unoptimized translation produced in the OSSA (Ownership SSA) form. **Canonical** SIL is the version after mandatory passes verify, simplify, and prepare the code for optimization.
- By generating SIL in OSSA form, the compiler explicitly tracks ownership of every value from the start, enabling more effective memory management optimizations and early bug detection.
- The final stage of the pipeline employs the LLVM framework. Optimized SIL is lowered into LLVM IR, a hardware-independent representation that LLVM then optimizes for the target hardware.

- The LLVM backend performs low-level optimizations such as instruction scheduling and register allocation before generating the final machine code that runs on the target CPU architecture (e.g., ARM64 on an iPhone).
- You can examine the compiler's output using the `swiftc` flags. The most helpful are `-emit-silgen` for raw SIL, `-emit-sil -Onone` for unoptimized canonical SIL, and `-emit-sil -O` for the final optimized SIL.
- Comparing unoptimized and optimized SIL visually demonstrates the effect of devirtualization. A dynamic `witness_method` call in the unoptimized version is often replaced by a direct `function_ref` or is fully inlined in the optimized version.
- Raw SIL in OSSA form exposes the hidden cost of Automatic Reference Counting. Instructions like `begin_borrow`, `end_borrow`, and `destroy_value` clearly illustrate how the compiler manages the lifetimes of your class instances.
- Understanding compiler errors is a skill. An error such as "generic parameter could not be inferred" indicates that the type checker lacks context, which is usually resolved by adding an explicit type annotation.
- The `-Xfrontend -debug-time-function-bodies` flag is a helpful tool for diagnosing slow compile times. It instructs the compiler to measure the time required to type-check each function, thereby aiding the identification of bottlenecks.
- Special attributes like `@inlinable` and `@_specialize` serve as direct instructions to the compiler, enabling you to influence its optimization decisions, which is essential for creating high-performance libraries.
- By default, a function's body is hidden outside its module. Marking a public function with `@inlinable` exposes its implementation, allowing other modules to inline it and reduce function-call overhead.
- Though `@_specialize` is an unofficial attribute, it instructs the compiler to generate and export a specialized, non-generic version of a function for specific types. This enables users of your library to link directly to a fast, pre-optimized implementation, bypassing dynamic dispatch.

Where to Go From Here?

In this chapter, you explored the compiler's black box. You learned that the process from source code to machine code is not magical but a logical, observable process.

The next step is to apply these insights to your everyday work. When you write a generic function, you'll now have a clear picture of the specialization and devirtualization that make it faster. When you choose between a struct and a class, you'll be able to visualize the invisible ARC traffic.

The true essence of this chapter is not memorizing SIL instructions but gaining a deeper intuition for the language. This knowledge should become your new superpower for debugging obscure performance issues and writing code that works with the compiler rather than against it.

Chapter 6: Unsafe Swift

Aaqib Hussain

What comes to mind when you hear the term "Unsafe Swift"? Do you picture a dark alley where pointers mug you for your memory addresses? Do you imagine some code written by a developer who wears sunglasses indoors? Or maybe just spaghetti code that crashes if you look at it wrong? Is it bad, poorly documented, or simply chaotic code? Surprisingly, Unsafe Swift isn't about writing bad code, but rather about using lower-level APIs to build tools for critical performance tasks. It is key to achieving peak performance in domains such as systems programming and data processing, and it is essential for smooth interoperability with C libraries.

You can understand this by analogy: think of **Safe Swift** as a modern car equipped with airbags, automatic braking, and lane assist. It keeps you safe automatically. Conversely, think of **Unsafe Swift** as a fast car with a manual transmission and no driver aids. It's incredibly fast and gives you direct control, but you are now solely responsible for staying on the track. You've intentionally removed the safety net.

Why would you purposefully do this? Sometimes, Swift's safety checks, such as ARC or array bounds checking, can introduce bottlenecks. In such rare cases, you can drop down to Unsafe Swift. It enables you to work directly with pointers, perform manual memory allocation, and manipulate raw bytes with minimal overhead.

This chapter aims to give you the keys to that *racecar*. It will introduce you to pointers, explain the lifecycle of manual memory management, explore byte-level operations, and deliver clear guidance on when (and, more importantly, when not) to depart from standard Swift.

The Meaning of Unsafe

Before you get the keys to that risky fast car, it's important to understand exactly what makes it unsafe. It isn't inherently bad or dangerous code; it's about responsibility. In normal, safe Swift, the compiler acts like a careful co-pilot, constantly checking your mirrors, assisting with lane changes, and keeping you aware of your speed, sometimes even taking control to prevent a crash. When you enter the world of Unsafe Swift, that co-pilot grabs a parachute and jumps out, yelling, "Good luck! You're on your own!" You are now fully in charge. If you drive off a cliff, the compiler won't stop you; it will just quietly admire your trajectory.

What Safety Does Swift Normally Guarantee?

That co-pilot helps prevent entire categories of common programming errors, especially those related to memory. To recap, the main safety features your compiler normally provides include:

- **Automatic Memory Management (ARC)**: You almost never have to think about allocating or deallocating memory for class instances. ARC automatically inserts `retain` and `release` calls to keep the objects alive until they are no longer needed, preventing memory leaks and dangling pointers.
- **Guaranteed Initialization**: The compiler also ensures that all your variables are initialized before use. This prevents you from accidentally using uninitialized variables, which could cause crashes or data discrepancies.
- **Bounds Checking**: When you access an `Array` or another `Collection` using an index in Swift, Swift checks if that index is valid. If it's out of bounds, it crashes your app predictably with an "index out of bounds" error instead of silently corrupting memory.
- **Strict Type Safety**: Swift is a strongly typed language. This helps prevent assigning an `Int` to a `String` type.

Features like these make Swift a safe and productive language to work with. They eliminate many low-level issues that can cause problems in languages like C/C++.

What Unsafe Really Means

So, what happens when you use APIs with **Unsafe** in their name, like `UnsafePointer`? It means the compiler steps back and lets you take the lead. It trusts you to manage the safety aspects it normally handles. **Unsafe** means *your responsibility*. You're telling the compiler: "Don't worry, I know what I'm doing here; turn off the usual safety checks."

Here are some guarantees that are no longer provided when working with Unsafe constructs:

- **No Automatic Memory Management**: If you manually allocate memory using unsafe pointers, you're responsible for deallocating it properly. Forgetting this may lead to memory leaks, and freeing it too early can also cause crashes.
- **No Guaranteed Initialization**: Memory allocated with unsafe APIs is just raw, uninitialized bytes. Reading from it before writing a valid value results in undefined behavior.
- **No Bounds Checking**: When you perform arithmetic, the compiler doesn't verify if you're moving past the end of the allocated memory. Accessing memory outside your bounds can cause crashes or subtle data corruption.
- **Ability to Violate Type Safety**: You can reinterpret blocks of memory with Unsafe APIs. For example, you might hold an `Int` in a variable and assign a `Float` to it at different times later. If done incorrectly, this can lead to nonsensical results or crashes.

Using Unsafe Swift means operating without the compiler's safety nets. It demands extra attention, careful consideration, and a thorough understanding of memory management principles.

The Pointer Family: Your Toolkit for Raw Memory

Just as painters need various brushes and pencils to create different shapes and designs, Unsafe Swift provides a family of pointer types, each created for a specific kind of memory access. Swift offers two categories: **typed pointers** and **raw pointers**.

Typed vs Raw Pointers

You can think of memory as a large warehouse filled with boxes.

- **Typed Pointers (`UnsafePointer<T>`, `UnsafeMutablePointer<T>`)**: These are like labeled boxes. You know precisely what is inside the box (for example, "Box contains Int" or "Box contains UserProfile"). These pointers see the data type they point to. This helps the compiler access your data correctly. You use typed pointers when you know the specific type of data you're working with.
- **Raw Pointers (`UnsafeRawPointer`, `UnsafeMutableRawPointer`)**: These are like boxes with only identification numbers labeled on them, making them easy to locate. You aren't aware of their contents. They are simply memory pointers without any associated type information. You use raw pointers when dealing with raw bytes, such as when interfacing with C code that uses `void *` or when you need to interpret bytes manually, for example, when reading or writing a file or handling data from a network socket.

The Four Main Pointer Types

Swift offers four main pointer types, representing combinations of typed/raw and mutable/immutable access:

Type	Access	Knows Type?	Description
`UnsafePointer<T>`	Read-Only	Yes	Points to memory containing type T. Cannot modify.
`UnsafeMutablePointer<T>`	Read/Write	Yes	Points to memory containing type T. Can modify.
`UnsafeRawPointer`	Read-Only	No	Points to raw memory bytes. Cannot modify.
`UnsafeMutableRawPointer`	Read/Write	No	Points to raw memory bytes. Can modify.

Swift Pointer Reference Guide

Key Points

- **Mutability**: Mutable versions allow you to change the memory the pointer references, whereas non-mutable versions allow only reading.
- **Type Safety**: Typed pointers (<T>) ensure safety because they know the size and layout of data. Raw pointers provide maximum flexibility but require manual handling of type interpretation.

Choosing the right pointer type is the key first step to effectively using Unsafe Swift. You select the tool that exactly fits the type of memory access you need; nothing more, nothing less.

Working with Typed Pointers

Typed pointers, `UnsafePointer<T>` and `UnsafeMutablePointer<T>`, are similar to possessing a detailed map that not only shows you *where* the data is but also *what* the data is. The `<T>` indicates the type (such as an `Int`, `Float`, or another type), which helps the compiler understand the layout and size of the memory location. The `Mutable` version allows you to modify the data, whereas the standard `UnsafePointer` is read-only.

Getting a Pointer to Existing Data

Generally, you won't need to manually allocate memory. In some cases, you might want to access the memory address of an existing variable, perhaps to pass it to a C function. Swift provides a safe, scoped way to do this: `withUnsafePointer(to:)` (and its mutable version, `withUnsafeMutablePointer(to:)`).

Consider you have a variable:

```
var score: Int = 100
```

To get a temporary pointer to its memory location:

```
withUnsafePointer(to: score) { pointer in
  // Inside this closure, 'pointer' is a valid
UnsafePointer<Int>
  // pointing directly to the memory where 'score' is stored.
  print("The memory address of score is: \(pointer)")
  print("The value stored at that address is: \
(pointer.pointee)")
```

```
    // You might pass 'pointer' to a C function here.
    // legacy_c_function(pointer)
}
```

Why is this safer? Swift ensures that the variable `score` is valid and that its memory isn't deallocated, modified, or moved while the closure is active. This prevents **dangling pointers** (pointers that refer to memory that no longer exists), which are a major source of crashes in languages like C. In Swift, creating long-lived pointers to a variable can be tricky and dangerous because Swift ensures those pointers remain valid for the duration of the function call. The memory may be freed or moved immediately afterward.

Manual Memory Management

Sometimes, especially when working with large amounts of data or performance-critical code, you need to manage memory yourself. This involves taking full control over the allocation and deallocation processes. It's like building your own house from scratch instead of buying one. While it gives you total control, it also comes with full responsibility. This lifecycle has four key steps: **Allocate**, **Initialize**, **Deinitialize**, and **Deallocate**.

Step 1: Allocate

First, you allocate a block of raw memory using `UnsafeMutablePointer<T>.allocate(capacity:)`. The capacity specifies the number of instances of type `T` you want to store.

```
let intPointer = UnsafeMutablePointer<Int>.allocate(capacity: 5)
```

Critical Warning: The pointer is just raw, uninitialized bytes. It doesn't contain any valid `Int` instances yet. Reading from this memory before initializing results in undefined behavior and may return garbage data.

Step 2: Initialize

Next, you must explicitly initialize the allocated memory. You fill the raw bytes with valid instances of your type `T`.

```
// Initialize
intPointer.initialize(from: [10, 20, 30, 40, 50], count: 5)

// The memory block contains [10, 20, 30, 40, 50]
print(intPointer.pointee)
```

Only after calling `.initialize` is it safe to read from the pointer using `.pointee`.

Step 3 & 4: Deinitialize and Deallocate

This is the most crucial part, helping prevent memory leaks and ensuring proper cleanup. When you're finished using memory, ensure you clean up in the same order the lifecycle requires: deinitialize, then deallocate.

```
// Assuming you allocated memory for 5 Ints earlier...

// 1. Deinitialize the 5 Ints
intPointer.deinitialize(count: 5)

// 2. Deallocate the raw memory block
intPointer.deallocate()
```

1. **Deinitialize**: If your type `T` is a class or has complex cleanup logic, you must call `.deinitialize(count:)`. This executes `deinit` logic for each instance stored in the memory block. For simple primitive types, this step might not do much, but it is essential for correctness with complex types.
2. **Deallocate**: Finally, you call `.deallocate()` to free the raw memory block back to the system.

Neglecting these steps, especially `.deallocate()`, can cause memory leaks. The memory remains allocated but unreachable, using resources until the app terminates.

To visualize the strict sequence of operations you must maintain, here is the complete manual memory management workflow:

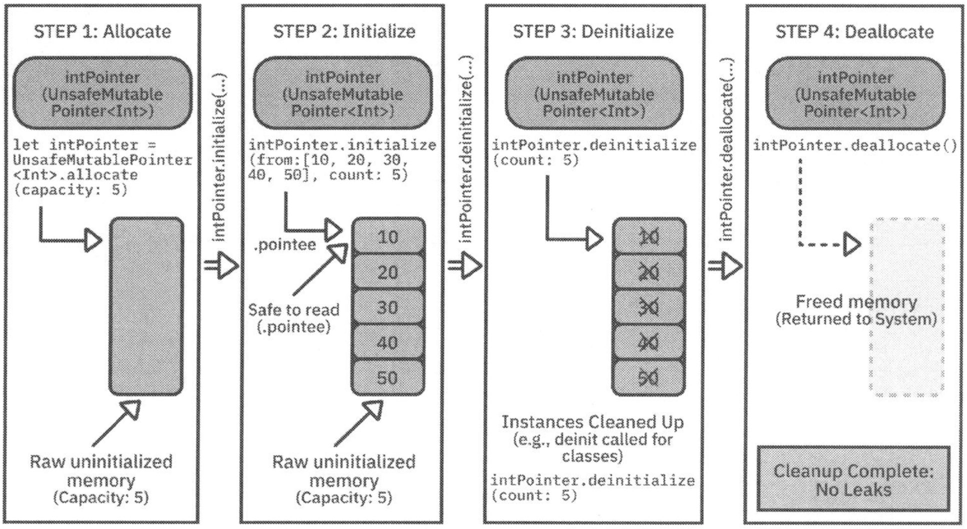

The Unsafe Pointer Lifecycle: Allocate, Initialize, Deinitialize, Deallocate

Pointer Arithmetic

When you allocate memory with a capacity greater than 1, you receive the initial pointer to the contiguous block of memory. From there, you can use pointer arithmetic to move to other memory locations.

Swift allows you to directly use + or – operators on typed pointers. Adding `n` to a pointer advances it by `n * MemoryLayout<T>.stride` bytes, pointing it exactly to the start of the `n`-th element.

```
let intPointer = UnsafeMutablePointer<Int>.allocate(capacity: 3)
intPointer.initialize(to: 100)
(intPointer + 1).initialize(to: 200) // Move to the next Int
location
(intPointer + 2).initialize(to: 300) // Move to the third Int
location

// Accessing the values
let firstValue = intPointer.pointee         // 100
let secondValue = (intPointer + 1).pointee // 200

// You can also use subscripting for convenience
let thirdValue = intPointer[2]              // 300 (equivalent
```

```
to (intPointer + 2).pointee)

// Don't forget to clean up!
intPointer.deinitialize(count: 3)
intPointer.deallocate()
```

The `.advanced(by: n)` method provides the same functionality as the + operator.

The following illustration depicts the overall concept and highlights the boundary that can lead to **undefined behavior**:

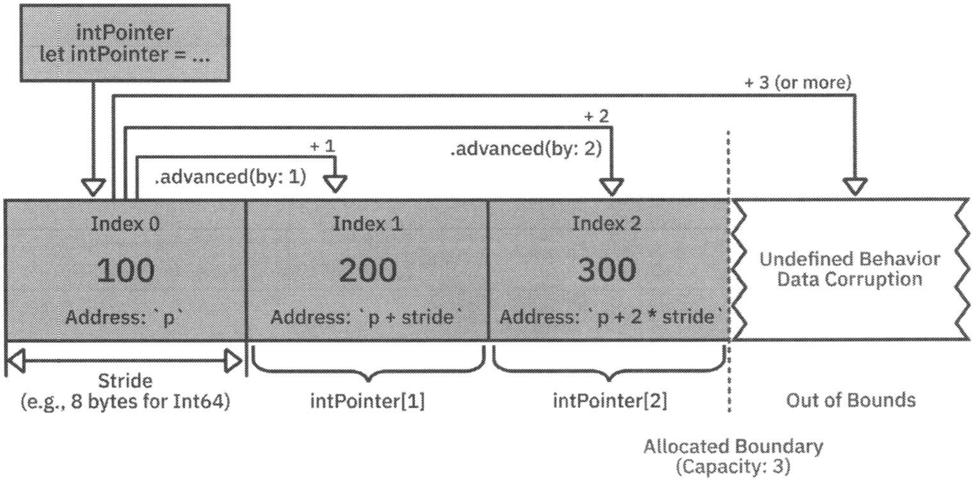

Stride, Capacity, and Undefined Behavior

> **Safety Note**: Pointer arithmetic does not include bounds checking. Accessing memory outside its allocated bounds can lead to corrupted data, security vulnerabilities, and may cause crashes. You are responsible for tracking capacity and ensuring you do not exceed the bounds.

Working with Buffers (UnsafeBufferPointer)

Pointer arithmetic allows direct control over moving between memory blocks; however, manually calculating offsets can lead to mistakes. A single misplaced `+ 1` can cause you to read or write outside the allocated bounds. For safer access to a continuous block of memory, similar to what you get with `.allocate(capacity:)`, Swift provides a more structured approach: `UnsafeBufferPointer` and its mutable version, `UnsafeMutableBufferPointer`.

These types serve as wrappers or views onto a memory region. They combine the starting pointer and the count, effectively representing a raw memory block as if it were a Swift `Collection`. This feature makes it easier to work with raw memory the Swift way, rather than relying on raw pointer arithmetic.

Creating a Buffer Pointer

You generally create a buffer pointer directly from a typed pointer that you've already allocated and initialized.

```
let capacity = 5
let intPointer = UnsafeMutablePointer<Int>.allocate(capacity:
capacity)
intPointer.initialize(repeating: 0, count: capacity) //
Initialize all elements

// Create a buffer pointer view onto this memory
let buffer = UnsafeMutableBufferPointer(start: intPointer,
count: capacity)

// IMPORTANT: The buffer pointer does NOT own the memory.
// It's just a temporary view. You are still responsible for
// deinitializing and deallocating the original `intPointer`.
defer {
  intPointer.deinitialize(count: capacity)
  intPointer.deallocate()
}
```

The buffer simply offers a safer interface to the memory managed by `intPointer`.

Safe Iteration and Access

The main benefit of `UnsafeBufferPointer` is that it implements `Collection` protocol. This allows you to use many of the safe, standard Swift APIs you're already familiar with.

```
// Use a standard for-in loop
for i in 0..<buffer.count {
  buffer[i] = i * 10 // Safe subscript access
}

// Iterate using for-in
for element in buffer {
  print(element)
}

// Use other Collection APIs
print("First element: \(buffer.first ?? -1)")
print("Contains 30: \(buffer.contains(30))")
```

Using the buffer pointer's `Collection` methods helps prevent accidental overstepping of the buffer's defined count, but remember that you are still responsible for managing the underlying memory. The buffer pointer does not use ARC and does not automatically deinitialize or deallocate the memory.

Passing Buffers to Functions

When an API requires efficient, read-only access to a contiguous memory block without copying it into a standard `Array`, `UnsafeBufferPointer` is often used as a function parameter. For example, a function that processes audio samples might accept an `UnsafeBufferPointer<Float>`. This allows the caller to access the raw sample data directly, thereby avoiding potentially expensive copies.

Using `UnsafeBufferPointer` adds an extra layer of safety when working with manually managed memory blocks, while also bridging the gap between raw pointer operations and Swift's safer collection handling methods.

Raw Pointers and Byte-Level Operations

Raw pointers (`UnsafeRawPointer` and `UnsafeMutableRawPointer`) are memory addresses without any attached type information, unlike their typed counterparts. The compiler treats them as opaque memory locations, leaving it to you to interpret the raw bytes correctly. This provides maximum flexibility but also means you are fully responsible for type safety and memory management.

When to Use Raw Pointers

Despite the risks involved, why would you ever use raw pointers? There are two main, valid scenarios in which they are necessary.

1. **Interacting with C APIs**: Many C functions use `void *` pointers as a generic way to pass around memory addresses without specifying the type. When these functions are imported into Swift, `void *` maps to `UnsafeRawPointer` or `UnsafeMutableRawPointer`. To work with these C APIs properly, you need to use Swift's raw pointer types.

2. **Direct Byte Operations**: Sometimes, you need to work directly with raw bytes, bypassing Swift's type system. This is common in low-level code, such as:

- **Networking**: Reading raw data packets from a socket.
- **File I/O**: Parsing custom binary file formats.

- **Low-Level Data Structures**: Creating custom memory allocators or specialized collections that pack data tightly.

In these cases, you treat memory as a sequence of bytes and are responsible for interpreting them according to the specific format or protocol you are working with.

Loading and Storing Typed Data

The most common use of raw pointers is to read or write typed data to or from raw memory. Swift provides several methods that require you to specify the data type you expect to access or store.

Loading Data

To read a value of a specific type `T` from raw memory, you use the `load(fromByteOffset:as:)` method. You specify the byte offset from the pointer's start and the type you want to read.

```
let rawPointer: UnsafeRawPointer = // ... Points to some memory

// Load the Int
let value = rawPointer.load(fromByteOffset: 0, as: Int.self)

print(value)
```

Alternatively, you can use the `load(as:)` method to load the value referenced by `rawPointer`.

Safety Considerations: This operation is very unsafe if done incorrectly:

Alignment: The memory address you're loading from (rawPointer + offset) must be aligned appropriately for type `T`. Loading an `Int` from an unaligned address can cause a crash.

Type: The bytes at that memory location must actually represent a valid instance of type `T`. Loading random bytes as though they were a `String` will likely cause a crash.

Initialization: The memory must be properly initialized.

Storing Data

To write raw bytes of a specific value into a raw memory location, use the `storeBytes(of:toByteOffset:as:)` method on `UnsafeMutableRawPointer`.

```
// A number to store
```

```
let myNumber = 42

// Assume you have a raw pointer to some memory
let rawPointer = UnsafeMutableRawPointer.allocate(
  byteCount: MemoryLayout<Int>.size,
  alignment: MemoryLayout<Int>.alignment
)
// Deallocate when done
defer { rawPointer.deallocate() }

// This copies the bytes of 'myNumber' into the allocated
memory.
rawPointer.storeBytes(of: myNumber, toByteOffset: 0, as:
Int.self)

// Load the Int
let value = rawPointer.load(as: Int.self)

print(value) // 42
```

Safety Considerations: Similar to `load`, you must verify that the pointer is valid, the offset is correct, and the memory region is large enough to hold the type's bytes you are storing.

Binding and Rebinding Memory

Raw pointers are simply addresses. To manipulate the memory they point to using typed pointer operations (`pointee` or pointer arithmetic), you need to inform Swift of the data type stored there. This process is called **memory binding**.

Type Punning

Type punning is the process of interpreting the same block of memory as a different type. For example, consider a sequence of bits in memory: `01000001`. If you interpret it as an unsigned integer, it equals 65. If you interpret it as ASCII, it represents the letter 'A'. While type punning is a powerful feature, it can be dangerous when misused, potentially causing crashes and data anomalies. Swift's binding APIs offer controlled methods for handling type punning.

Memory bound to a type can be rebound to a different type only after it has been deinitialized, or if the bound type is trivial. Deinitializing typed memory doesn't unbind the memory's type; it only destroys the instance stored there. This memory can then be reinitialized with values of the same type or even bound to a new type.

Trivial type:Swift native types that are independent of indirection and reference counting are considered trivial types. Examples include integers (`Int`, `UInt8`), floating-point numbers (`Float`, `Double`), and `Bool`. In C, structs and enumerations composed solely of trivial types are also classified as trivial.

The `bindMemory(to:capacity:)` method establishes a lasting association between the raw memory and the type being stored. You're essentially telling the compiler: "Treat this block of memory, starting from this address and extending over the `capacity` elements, as if it contains instances of type `T`."

```
let byteCount = 3 * MemoryLayout<Int>.stride
let alignment = MemoryLayout<Int>.alignment
let rawPointer = UnsafeMutableRawPointer.allocate(byteCount:
byteCount, alignment: alignment)
defer { rawPointer.deallocate() }

// Bind the raw memory to Int. This returns a typed pointer.
let typedPointer = rawPointer.bindMemory(to: Int.self, capacity:
3)

// Now you can work with it like a normal typed pointer
typedPointer.initialize(to: 10)
(typedPointer + 1).initialize(to: 20)
typedPointer[2] = 30 // Using subscript after initialization

print(typedPointer[1]) // Output: 20

// IMPORTANT: Deinitialize using the typed pointer BEFORE
deallocating the raw pointer
typedPointer.deinitialize(count: 3)
```

Strict Rules: Memory binding has very strict rules:

1. Memory should only be bound to one data type at a time.
2. The type you bind to (`T`) must match the actual data type you plan to store.
3. Make sure the memory is properly aligned for `T`.

`withMemoryRebound(to:capacity:)` is a much safer, temporary, and scoped way to perform type punning. It's mainly used when working with C APIs that expect a different but layout-compatible type from the one you have.

Imagine you have a pointer to `Int8` (signed bytes), but you need to pass it to a C function that expects a pointer to `UInt8` (unsigned bytes), since `Int8` and `UInt8` have the same size and alignment.

```
func processSignedBytes(_ bytes: UnsafePointer<Int8>, count:
Int) {
  print("Processing signed bytes...")

  // Temporarily 'rebound' the memory to UInt8 within this scope
  bytes.withMemoryRebound(to: UInt8.self, capacity: count)
{ unsignedBytesPointer in
    // Inside this closure, 'unsignedBytesPointer' is an
UnsafePointer<UInt8>
    // pointing to the exact same memory location as 'bytes'.

    // Call a C function that expects unsigned bytes
    // some_c_function(unsignedBytesPointer, count)
    print("Called C function with pointer: \
(unsignedBytesPointer)")
  }

  // Outside the closure, the pointer is back to being
UnsafePointer<Int8>.
}

// Example usage
let signedData: [Int8] = [-1, 0, 1, 127]
signedData.withUnsafeBufferPointer { bufferPointer in
  processSignedBytes(bufferPointer.baseAddress!, count:
bufferPointer.count)
}
```

Safety: `withMemoryRebound` is safer because the type change is temporary and scoped. However, it still requires that the involved types (`Int8` and `UInt8`) have the same size and compatible alignment. Rebinding memory to an unrelated type results in undefined behavior.

Raw pointers provide the ultimate control over memory but require the most discipline. Use them only when absolutely necessary and always verify alignment, initialization, and type compatibility.

The Why and When: Practical Guidance

The tools Unsafe Swift provides are powerful and not limited to pointers for direct memory access, manual memory management, and reinterpretation of raw bytes. You're also aware of the effects it can have on your code. As Uncle Ben once said: "With great power comes great responsibility."

Before you dive into using `UnsafePointer`, it's critical to understand the principles governing its appropriate use. When do the benefits outweigh the risks?

The Golden Rule: Avoid Unsafe Swift if Possible

To clarify, using Unsafe Swift should be a last resort. Most of your code should rely on Swift's safe, idiomatic constructs. The safety checks provided by the compiler and ARC are there for a reason. These features help eliminate entire classes of bugs that have troubled developers for decades.

Before opting for an `UnsafePointer`, always ask yourself:

1. Can I accomplish this with Swift's built-in data types?
2. Can standard library methods or existing features solve my problem?
3. Is the performance bottleneck confirmed through profiling, and is it significant enough to justify the added complexity and risk?

If a solution using Swift's built-in features exists, it is always the better choice for maintainability, readability, long-term stability, and to avoid unnecessary knowledge transfer challenges for new developers.

Legitimate Use Case 1: C Interoperability

The most common and unquestionably important use of Unsafe Swift is interoperating with C libraries. C APIs frequently use pointers (*) to pass data, especially for `inout` parameters or when working with memory buffers. Swift's Clang importer often maps these to Swift's `UnsafePointer` family.

Swift's `withUnsafePointer(to:)` (and its mutable versions) is specifically designed for this purpose. They offer a safe, temporary bridge between Swift's memory-managed environment and C's raw pointer interface.

Imagine you need to call a C function that calculates the dimensions of a rectangle, which takes pointers to `Doubles` to store the width and height results.

```
// C header file
typedef struct { double x, y; } CPoint;
void calculateDimensions(CPoint topLeft, CPoint bottomRight,
double *widthOut, double *heightOut);
```

In Swift, you would call this function safely like this:

```
struct Point { // Your Swift struct
  var x, y: Double
}
```

```
let topLeft = Point(x: 10, y: 20)
let bottomRight = Point(x: 110, y: 70)

var calculatedWidth: Double = 0.0
var calculatedHeight: Double = 0.0

// Use withUnsafeMutablePointer to safely pass addresses to C
withUnsafeMutablePointer(to: &calculatedWidth) { widthPointer in
  withUnsafeMutablePointer(to: &calculatedHeight)
{ heightPointer in
    let cTopLeft = CPoint(x: topLeft.x, y: topLeft.y)
    let cBottomRight = CPoint(x: bottomRight.x, y:
bottomRight.y)

    // Call the C function with the temporary, valid pointers
    calculateDimensions(cTopLeft, cBottomRight, widthPointer,
heightPointer)
  }
}

// After the closures, the C function has written the results
// directly into the Swift variables.
print("Calculated Width: \(calculatedWidth)")
print("Calculated Height: \(calculatedHeight)")
```

This is an ideal example: `withUnsafeMutablePointer` provides temporary, guaranteed-valid pointers for C functions to use, without exposing users to the risks of managing long-lived pointers across the language boundary.

Legitimate Use Case 2: Performance-Critical Code

The primary reason for using Unsafe Swift is performance. While Swift's safety features are valuable, they are not free and can impose a performance cost. Built-in features like array bounds checks, ARC retain and release calls, and abstraction overhead can accumulate in highly performance-sensitive code.

When might this occur?

- **Custom Data Structures**: When building a highly specialized data structure (such as a B-tree, deque, or custom memory pool) for which standard library types fall short, manual memory management can yield significantly better performance by precisely controlling memory layout and avoiding ARC.

- **Low-Level Processing**: In fields like gaming, high-level physics simulations, rendering graphics, audio/video processing, or certain computing tasks, you may encounter tight loops that handle large amounts of data. In these cases, removing ARC or array-bound checks and working directly with pointers to pre-allocated memory buffers can produce remarkable results.

- **Minimal Abstraction Cost**: Sometimes, you need to ensure your code compiles into the most efficient machine instructions without hidden costs from protocols or generics. Dropping down to raw pointers can accomplish this, but it requires deep expertise.

Hypothetical Example: Imagine you're processing audio in real-time. You might receive raw audio in a large `Data` buffer. Copying this into a Swift array could be too slow. Instead, you could use `Data.withUnsafeBytes` to get a raw pointer to the underlying buffer and process the audio samples directly in-place using pointer arithmetic.

> **Note**: This path should only be taken after profiling your application and demonstrating that using raw pointers is the only feasible solution. Premature optimization with Unsafe Swift is a recipe for disaster and can lead to error-prone code if used carelessly.

Key Points

- Unsafe Swift isn't about writing poor-quality code. It is a powerful, low-level toolset designed for two specific purposes: high-performance, systems-level programming and seamless interoperability with C libraries.

- Swift safeguards you from entire categories of bugs by offering ARC, guaranteed variable initialization, array bounds checking, and strict type safety.

- **Unsafe** means "your responsibility." By using these APIs, you are instructing the compiler to disable its safety features, and you are now entirely responsible for handling memory and type safety.

- The pointer family is divided into two main groups. Typed pointers (such as `UnsafePointer<T>`) are aware of the data type they point to, while raw pointers (like `UnsafeRawPointer`) are untyped memory addresses, similar to C's `void *`.

- The four main types cover all access needs: UnsafePointer<T> (read-only, typed), UnsafeMutablePointer<T> (read-write, typed), UnsafeRawPointer (read-only, raw), and UnsafeMutableRawPointer (read-write, raw).
- The safest way to get a pointer to an existing Swift variable is within a scoped closure using withUnsafePointer(to:). This guarantees that the pointer is valid only within that scope, preventing dangling pointers.
- Always pair allocate() with deallocate() and initialize() with deinitialize(count:) to prevent memory leaks. Forgetting to deallocate can cause memory to be held for the entire lifetime of your app.
- You can use + or .advanced(by:) to move typed pointers. This is unsafe because the compiler does not verify whether you are moving past the end of your allocated memory block. You are responsible for tracking the capacity.
- To handle a contiguous block of memory more safely, wrap it in an UnsafeBufferPointer. This provides a collection-like interface with safe subscripts (buffer[i]) and for...in loops, but you still need to manage the memory's lifecycle.
- Raw pointers use load(as:) to read a typed value (like an Int) from a raw byte address and storeBytes(of:toByteOffset:as:) to write the bytes of a value into raw memory. You are responsible for ensuring the correct type, alignment, and initialization.
- **Type punning** involves interpreting raw memory as a particular type. bindMemory(to:capacity:) is a one-time operation that instructs Swift to permanently treat a block of raw memory as a specific typed pointer.
- The safer usage, scoped withMemoryRebound(to:capacity:), is for temporarily treating a pointer as a different type, such as converting an UnsafePointer<Int8> to an UnsafePointer<UInt8> to pass to a C API. This is only safe for layout-compatible types.
- Use Unsafe Swift only as a last resort. Always prioritize safe, idiomatic Swift. Consider unsafe APIs only after profiling your application and confirming that a safe implementation would introduce a significant performance issue.
- The two main, legitimate uses for Unsafe Swift are interfacing with C libraries that require pointers and writing highly optimized, performance-critical code (e.g., custom data structures, game physics, or low-level parsing).

Where to Go From Here?

You've explored one of the most powerful features of the Swift language. You now hold the keys to the *racecar* and understand the responsibilities that come with it.

The next step isn't just about writing unsafe code, but about applying this knowledge to become a more capable and thoughtful Swift developer. When you create your next high-level API, you'll gain a deeper understanding of the costs associated with abstractions. When working with a C library, you'll do so confidently. And when faced with a truly challenging performance bottleneck, you'll have the full toolkit to address it.

You've completed your journey from high-level abstractions to raw bytes. This foundational knowledge is the final piece of the puzzle, enabling you to master Swift thoroughly.

Section III: Scalable Architecture & Tooling

This section teaches how to apply these low-level concepts at the system level. You'll learn metaprogramming techniques like reflection, result builders, and macros to reduce boilerplate and enforce consistency.

You'll also learn about modularization, static vs dynamic linking, Swift Package Manager internals, and dependency graphs. The focus is on structuring large codebases for faster builds, clear boundaries, predictable dependencies, and long-term maintainability.

Chapter 7: Metaprogramming

Aaqib Hussain

The word "meta" is actually a Greek term that is commonly used as a prefix today. It means "beyond" or "after." Metaprogramming refers to going "beyond" just writing code that runs. It's not about the app logic itself—like performing a network request, developing UI, or building business logic—but about the powerful practice of writing code that can **generate**, **analyze**, or **transform** another piece of code. This is where the Swift language becomes a tool to manipulate your codebase.

Why should you care? This is the ultimate weapon against boilerplate code. The repetitive code you copy-paste for equality conformance, JSON decoding, or test mocks is a major source of bugs and is difficult to maintain. Here, metaprogramming acts as a knight in shining armor, enabling you to write a single piece of code that generates other repetitive code, ensuring consistency from a single source of truth. It also powers the creation of expressive, human-readable Domain-Specific Languages (DSLs).

This chapter explores three distinct metaprogramming methods in Swift, each with its own trade-offs along the spectrum of runtime flexibility and compile-time safety. You'll start with runtime inspection using `Mirror`, which lets you peek inside any type while your app is running. Next, you'll learn about compile-time transformation with `@resultBuilder`, the engine that turns simple Swift into complex data structures. Finally, you'll gain hands-on experience with **Swift Macros**, a feature that generates code during compilation, eliminating entire categories of boilerplate with a single line. This chapter isn't about hammering nails; it's about building the hammer.

The Magic Mirror: Runtime Reflection with Mirror

In standard programming, you write code that operates on data. You are aware of the variables, their types, properties, and methods during compilation. But what if you want to see it while your code is running? What if you want to write a generic inspector that can examine any object? Whether it's a struct `User`, an enum `NetworkError`, or even a class you haven't implemented yet.

This is a common feature also available in languages other than Swift. It's called **Reflection**. It refers to a program's ability to inspect its structure such as types, relationships, and properties at runtime. In Swift, the primary tool to effectively leverage this capability is `Mirror`.

What is Reflection?

Reflection is a kind of metaprogramming that happens only at runtime. Unlike compilation tools that validate code before execution, reflection examines your app's objects in memory while they are active.

You can think of it as holding a mirror up to your code. Usually, a function only sees the values it's passed. With reflection, you can see the structure of those values and answer questions such as:

- What kind of thing are you? (A struct? A class? A tuple?)
- What are the names of your properties?
- What values are currently stored in those properties?

Swift intentionally limits reflection capabilities to preserve performance and type safety. Unlike Objective-C, Swift reflection does not allow method invocation, mutation, or dynamic type creation at runtime. However, `Mirror` offers a standardized, safe way to peek inside instances when you truly need that dynamic behavior.

How to Use Mirror?

Using a `Mirror` is quite simple. You create a `Mirror` to reflect any instance you want to inspect.

Consider the following code:

```
struct User {
  let name: String
  let age: Int
}

let michael = User(name: "Michael Scott", age: 44)

// Create the mirror
let mirror = Mirror(reflecting: michael)
```

Once you have the mirror object, one of its most useful properties is `children`. This is the collection of all visible parts of the reflected subject. Each child is a tuple containing an optional `label` (the property name) and a `value` (the stored data).

Iterating over the `children` collection:

```
print("Inspecting \(mirror.subjectType):")
for child in mirror.children {
  let propertyName = child.label ?? "unknown"
  print("  - \(propertyName): \(child.value)")
}
// Output:
// Inspecting User:
//   - name: Michael Scott
//   - age: 44
```

You can also identify the type of an object. It's an optional enum that can be `.struct`, `.class`, `.enum`, `.tuple`, `.optional`, `.collection`, and more, by using the `displayStyle` property on the `Mirror` object. It is important to be aware of the type you're dealing with when handling values. For example, you might want to format a `.class` differently than a `.tuple` in a logging tool.

Practical Use Case: Building a Generic prettyPrint

The best way to use `Mirror` is to create something useful with it. A common issue in debugging is printing complex objects, resulting in unreadable, jumbled output. You can use `Mirror` to write a generic function that uses reflection to recursively print any object with clear indentation.

This function doesn't need prior knowledge of the types it will print. It will use `Mirror` to figure it out dynamically.

Take a look at the function below:

```
func prettyPrint(_ value: Any, indent: Int = 0) {
    let mirror = Mirror(reflecting: value)

    // Base case: If the value has no children, just print the
it directly.
    if mirror.children.isEmpty {
        print(value)
        return
    }

    // Determine if it's a collection to use [] instead of ().
    let isCollection = mirror.displayStyle == .collection ||
mirror.displayStyle == .set || mirror.displayStyle
== .dictionary
    let open = isCollection ? "[" : "("
    let close = isCollection ? "]" : ")"

    // Print type name (if not a collection) and opening
bracket.
    if !isCollection {
        print("\(mirror.subjectType)", terminator: "")
    }
    print(open)

    let childIndent = String(repeating: "  ", count: indent + 1)

    for child in mirror.children {
        // Always print indentation first
        print(childIndent, terminator: "")

        // If it has a label (like struct properties), print it.
        // Arrays usually don't have labels for their elements.
        if let label = child.label {
            print("\(label): ", terminator: "")
        }
```

```
        // Recurse for the value
        prettyPrint(child.value, indent: indent + 1)
    }

    // Print closing bracket with parents' indentation.
    let footerIndent = String(repeating: "  ", count: indent)
    print("\(footerIndent)\(close)")
}
```

Now, you can pass anything to this function:

```
struct Company {
  let boss: User
  let employees: [User]
}

let dunderMifflin = Company(
  boss: User(name: "Michael", age: 44),
  employees: [
    User(name: "Jim", age: 33),
    User(name: "Dwight", age: 38)
  ]
)

prettyPrint(dunderMifflin)
```

The `prettyPrint` function implements recursion and utilizes `Mirror`. It will traverse deeply into the `Company` struct, locate the `boss` property, verify that it is of type `User`, and continue digging.

It yields the following output:

```
Company(
  boss: User(
    name: Michael
    age: 44
  )
  employees: [
    User(
      name: Jim
      age: 33
    )
    User(
      name: Dwight
      age: 38
    )
  ]
)
```

It's a powerful, versatile implementation built entirely on runtime introspection.

The Limitations of the Mirror

While `Mirror` is a phenomenal tool, it comes with important trade-offs, especially compared to reflection in more dynamic languages.

First and foremost, `Mirror` is read-only. You can inspect an object, read its property names, and get its values, but you cannot modify them. You cannot use `Mirror` to set new values for the `age` property of the `User` object or change its `name` property. Swift's strict emphasis on type safety and immutability prevents this kind of "backdoor" access.

Second, reflection is slow. Because it occurs entirely at runtime, it involves dynamic type checking, creating new collection wrappers for `children`, and boxing values into `Any`. It also prevents many compile-time optimizations that Swift normally relies on. While it's perfect for debugging, logging, or serialization, you should never use `Mirror` in performance-critical tasks. It is a heavy, dynamic tool in a language optimized for static performance.

Dynamic Lookups: @dynamicMemberLookup

`@dynamicMemberLookup` lets you intercept accesses to members that don't exist at compile time.

Normally in Swift, if you write `someInstance.someProperty` and `someProperty` doesn't exist, the compiler throws an error and stops you immediately. This is a core safety feature. But what about when you're working with inherently dynamic data, like JSON, where the keys are unknown until runtime? `@dynamicMemberLookup` makes this possible by letting you create clean, dot-syntax APIs over data that is inherently unstructured.

What is @dynamicMemberLookup?

`@dynamicMemberLookup` is an attribute that you can apply to a `struct`, `class`, or `enum`. It fundamentally alters how the compiler handles property access on that type.

When you apply this attribute, you're making a promise to the compiler. "Hey compiler, if you see someone try to access a property on this type that you don't recognize, don't throw an error. Instead, just trust me. At runtime, I will provide an implementation that handles that call." This lets you adopt dynamic behavior found in languages like Python or JavaScript, but in a controlled, explicit way.

Applying the @dynamicMemberLookup Attribute

To fulfill the promise with the compiler, the type marked with `@dynamicMemberLookup` must implement a special subscript method: `subscript(dynamicMember member: String)`. The `String` parameter represents the member name extracted from the dot syntax.

When the compiler encounters a dot-syntax access to an unresolved member, it rewrites that expression into a call to this subscript. That's where the compiler performs this magic translation.

Check the following example of using the `@dynamicMemberLookup` attribute on a dynamic dictionary.

```
@dynamicMemberLookup
struct DynamicDictionary {
  private var data: [String: Any]

  init(_ data: [String: Any]) {
    self.data = data
  }

  // The required subscript
  subscript(dynamicMember member: String) -> Any? {
    print("Dynamic lookup for member: '\(member)'")
    return data[member]
  }
}
```

Now you can call the properties like:

```
let user = DynamicDictionary(["name": "Jim Halpert", "age": 33])

// 1
let name = user.name
// 2
print(name)
```

A quick analysis of each line is as follows:

1. The dot syntax is available, and the compiler doesn't give you an error.
2. It prints:

- `Dynamic lookup for member: 'name'`
- `Optional("Jim Halpert")`

This compiler trick is fundamental to dynamic member lookup. It secretly converts simple dot-syntax (`user.name`) into string-based dictionary lookups (`user[dynamicMember: "name"]`), providing the best of both worlds.

Practical Use Case: A Type-Safe JSON Wrapper

The most common and powerful use case for a `@dynamicMemberLookup` is building a wrapper that makes JSON-style access cleaner and more ergonomic.

You should be aware of the **pyramid of doom**. The indentation gets so deep that you practically need a climbing rope and a headlamp to find your way back out. It's typically caused by nested casting when accessing dictionary values. The code usually looks like this:

```
// The "Before" - Painful, nested casting
var userName: String?
if let userDict = json["user"] as? [String: Any] {
  if let nameValue = userDict["name"] as? String {
    userName = nameValue
  }
}
```

This is difficult to read and very fragile. You can improve this by creating a `JSON` struct that wraps your data and uses `@dynamicMemberLookup` for a clean, chainable approach. Take a look at the code below:

```
@dynamicMemberLookup
struct JSON {
```

```
  private var data: Any?

  init(_ data: Any?) {
    self.data = data
  }

  subscript(dynamicMember member: String) -> JSON {
    guard let dict = data as? [String: Any] else {
      return JSON(nil)
    }
    return JSON(dict[member])
  }

  var string: String? {
    return data as? String
  }

  var int: Int? {
    return data as? Int
  }

  var array: [JSON]? {
    guard let arr = data as? [Any] else { return nil }
    return arr.map { JSON($0) }
  }
}
```

Now, you can use this wrapper like this:

```
// The "After" - Clean, chainable, and readable
let userData: [String: Any] = [
  "user": [
    "name": "Michael G. Scott",
    "age": 44
  ]
]

let json = JSON(userData)
let name = json.user.name.string
print(name) // Prints Optional("Michael G. Scott")
```

To understand what is happening here:

1. `json.user`: The compiler cannot find the `user` property. It calls the `subscript(dynamicMember: "user")`. This retrieves the **user** object from the provided `userData` dictionary and returns a new `JSON` struct that wraps that dictionary.

2. `.name`: This is called on the new `JSON` struct. The compiler again calls `subscript(dynamicMember: "name")`. This finds the **name** property within the **user** object and returns a new `JSON` object containing only that string.
3. `.string`: This is a standard property call on the `JSON` struct. It attempts to cast its internal data (`"Michael G. Scott"`) to a `String` and returns it.

This is a great example of metaprogramming in practice: you built a tool that enables clean, chainable, API-like syntax while dynamically managing unstructured data at runtime.

The DSL Factory: Mastering Result Builders

Inspecting objects during runtime is interesting; what's even more exciting is working with powerful compile-time metaprogramming concepts. This is where the code's structure is modified as it's being compiled.

One of the most elegant and widely used examples in Swift is the **Result Builder** system. It's what makes SwiftUI APIs feel declarative and natural, and it allows you to build your own **Domain-Specific Languages (DSLs)** directly in Swift.

What is a Domain Specific Language (DSL)?

A **Domain Specific Language (DSL)** is a small language created for a specific task. Swift is a general-purpose language; you can use it to build anything, from watch apps to web servers. In contrast, a DSL is highly focused, offering a limited set of commands and a specific syntax that makes it very expressive for one particular domain.

A common example in the Apple ecosystem is SwiftUI. When you write a SwiftUI view, you're not writing typical imperative Swift, you're using a DSL.

Think about the difference. Without a DSL, you typically build UI hierarchies imperatively:

```
// The "old" way (imperative)
let text = Text("Hello")
let image = Image("icon")
let stack = VStack()
stack.addArrangedSubview(text)
stack.addArrangedSubview(image)
```

```
return stack
```

This feels awkward. You're concentrating on the *how*, creating instances and calling methods.

SwiftUI's DSL, powered by `@ViewBuilder`, allows you to write this declaratively:

```
// The DSL way (declarative)
VStack {
  Text("Hello")
  Image("icon")
}
```

This marks a significant shift in how you express intent. The code mirrors the hierarchy it creates: it's clean, readable, and emphasizes the what over the how. That's the goal of a good DSL—providing a high-level description of the desired outcome instead of a low-level sequence of steps that the reader must mentally reconstruct. You can see this pattern in HTML for document structure or SQL for database queries. In Swift, `@resultBuilder` is the attribute that enables you to craft these expressive mini-languages.

Introducing @resultBuilder

So how does a simple list of views become a complex, combined view? The answer you're looking for is the `@resultBuilder` attribute.

You use this attribute when declaring a `class`, `struct`, `enum`, or `actor`. It instructs the compiler: "When you encounter this attribute, apply a predefined set of transformation rules to the statements inside it." It's a transformer that the compiler uses to rewrite your code behind the scenes.

It takes a sequence of normal Swift statements and converts them, one by one, into a single combined value.

That beautiful, declarative SwiftUI code you wrote:

```
VStack {
  Text("Hello")
  Image("icon")
}
```

...is just syntactic sugar. Because `VStack`'s `content` parameter is marked with `@ViewBuilder`, the compiler actually sees this and rewrites it into something like this behind the scenes:

```
VStack(content: {
  let view1 = Text("Hello")
  let view2 = Image("icon")
  return ViewBuilder.buildBlock(view1, view2)
})
```

The purpose of the result builder is to implement a set of static methods (like `buildBlock`) that define how the statements passed to them are transformed. It's like a machine in a factory that takes in raw materials to produce a finished product.

Using a Result Builder: buildBlock

To grasp the concept of this attribute, you're going to build a simple example `ArrayBuilder` whose only job is to take a list of items and wrap them in an array.

First, define a builder `struct`.

```
@resultBuilder
struct ArrayBuilder<T> {
  // This is the most important method.
  // It takes a list of components and combines them.
  static func buildBlock(_ components: T...) -> [T] {
    print("buildBlock called with \(components.count) items")
    return components
  }
}
```

You've defined a builder, `ArrayBuilder`, and implemented the one static method it needs to combine multiple components: `buildBlock`. Now, create a function that uses this builder:

```
func buildArray<T>(@ArrayBuilder<T> content: () -> [T]) -> [T] {
  return content()
}

let numbers = buildArray {
  1
  2
  3
}

print(numbers)
```

When you run this, the console prints:

```
buildBlock called with 3 items
[1, 2, 3]
```

This demonstrates what the compiler did. It recognized the sequence of statements `1, 2, 3` inside the closure marked with `@ArrayBuilder` and converted it into a single function call: `ArrayBuilder.buildBlock(1, 2, 3)`. This `buildBlock` method is the core component of all result builders.

Adding Logic

A DSL that only supports static elements is limited. The real power of a result builder emerges when you add support for control flow, like `if` and `else` statements.

However, introducing logic creates a type challenge. In the previous example, you were just passing single items `T`. But an `if` statement might return a value, or might not return anything. To handle this variability cleanly, you apply a normalization strategy: convert everything to an array `[T]` before combining.

This requires the implementation of `buildExpression` to wrap single elements into arrays, and updating `buildBlock` to accept `[T]...` instead of single elements. Once the foundation is in place, you can implement control flows.

Handling `if` Statements

When you write `if condition { value }`, the compiler first runs the expression inside the branch through `buildExpression`, turning it into `[T]`. It then calls `buildOptional`.

Since the input is now an array, `buildOptional` receives `[T]?`. If the condition is false, the input is `nil`. You implement `buildOptional` to handle this by returning an empty array in the `nil` case, ensuring `buildBlock` always receives a valid list to flatten.

```
@resultBuilder
struct ArrayBuilder<T> {
  static func buildExpression(_ expression: T) -> [T] {
    print("buildExpression called")
    return [expression]
  }

  // 2. Accept variadic arrays and flatten them
  static func buildBlock(_ components: [T]...) -> [T] {
    print("buildBlock called with \(components.count) items")
    return components.flatMap { $0 }
  }

  // This enables: if condition { ... }
  static func buildOptional(_ component: [T]?) -> [T] {
    print("buildOptional called")
    return component ?? []
```

```
  }
}
```

Now, if you change your original code to the following:

```
var showExtra = false
let numbers = buildArray {
  1
  2
  if showExtra {
    3
  }
}
```

It prints in the console:

```
buildBlock called with 3 items
[1, 2]
```

Although the closure contains three statements, the final result includes only the elements from the branches that produced values.

Handling `if-else` Statements

For handling `if-else` or `switch` statements, two other functions come into play that the compiler uses: `func buildEither(first component: [T]) -> [T]` and `func buildEither(second component: [T]) -> [T]`. Again, because of normalization, these methods receive and return `[T]`.

They act as simple pass-through, satisfying the compiler's requirement to unify the types coming from different code branches into a single type that `buildBlock` can process.

```
static func buildEither(first component: [T]) -> [T] {
  return component
}

static func buildEither(second component: [T]) -> [T] {
  return component
}
```

It only works when all these methods: `buildExpression`, `buildBlock`, `buildOptional`, and `buildEither` are present and aligned on the `[T]` type that the compiler can successfully transform complex logic into a flat array.

```
@resultBuilder
struct ArrayBuilder<T> {
```

```
  // 1. Normalize single items to arrays
  static func buildExpression(_ expression: T) -> [T] {
    print("buildExpression called")
    return [expression]
  }

  // 2. Accept variadic arrays and flatten them
  static func buildBlock(_ components: [T]...) -> [T] {
    print("buildBlock called with \(components.count) items")
    return components.flatMap { $0 }
  }

  // 3. Logic methods must now work with [T]
  static func buildOptional(_ component: [T]?) -> [T] {
    return component ?? []
  }

  static func buildEither(first component: [T]) -> [T] { return
component }
  static func buildEither(second component: [T]) -> [T] { return
component }
}
```

Now, if you return to the `buildArray` function and include an `else` condition like this:

```
var showExtra = false
let numbers = buildArray {
  1
  2
  if showExtra {
    3
  } else {
    4
  }
}
```

You should see the console printing the following:

```
[1, 2, 4]
```

With these methods, `ArrayBuilder` can now handle full conditional logic, just like SwiftUI's `ViewBuilder`. It's a simpler builder compared to `ViewBuilder`. In `ViewBuilder`, these methods wrap the two different view types in a special internal `_ConditionalContent` view, ensuring the entire `if-else` expression resolves to a single, consistent type.

Practical Use Case: Building a Simple HTMLBuilder

You can use what you've learned about result builders and put it into practical use by developing an expressive DSL for generating HTML strings. The goal is to write Swift that reads like HTML.

Step 1: Define the Builder: The builder will build `String` components. The `buildBlock` function concatenates all the strings with newlines. Also, you add `buildEither` and `buildOptional` methods so you can use `if` and `else` statements.

```
@resultBuilder
struct HTMLBuilder {
  static func buildBlock(_ components: String...) -> String {
    components.joined(separator: "\n")
  }

  static func buildOptional(_ component: String?) -> String {
    component ?? ""
  }

  static func buildEither(first component: String) -> String
{ component }
  static func buildEither(second component: String) -> String
{ component }
}
```

Step 2: Define Helper Functions: You'll create helper functions that wrap content in HTML tags. These functions form the vocabulary of your DSL.

```
func html(@HTMLBuilder content: () -> String) -> String {
  "<html>\n\(content())\n</html>"
}

func body(@HTMLBuilder content: () -> String) -> String {
  "<body>\n\(content())\n</body>"
}

func p(_ content: String) -> String {
  "<p>\(content)</p>"
}

func h1(_ content: String) -> String {
  "<h1>\(content)</h1>"
}
```

Note that `html` and `body` annotate their closure parameters with `@HTMLBuilder`, enabling the multi-statement DSL syntax inside those closures.

Step 3: Use the DSL: You can now write clear, declarative code to generate an HTML document.

You can use it like this:

```
let isLoggedIn = true

let myPage = html {
  body {
    h1("Welcome to our site!")
    if isLoggedIn {
      p("You are logged in.")
    } else {
      p("Please log in to continue.")
    }
    p("This is a DSL-powered website.")
  }
}

print(myPage)
```

It produces an HTML string like this:

```
<html>
<body>
<h1>Welcome to our site!</h1>
<p>You are logged in.</p>
<p>This is a DSL-powered website.</p>
</body>
</html>
```

This demonstrates the power of result builders. You've designed a compile-time transformation system that turns readable Swift into a structured HTML string. You've built the factory, now you can use it to produce consistent output with a clean call site.

The New Frontier: Swift Macros

For years, Swift developers have chased the Holy Grail of clean code: eliminating boilerplate. In pursuit of this, they have used inheritance, protocol extensions, and generic constraints to reduce repetition. Yet, you still find yourself writing `CodingKeys` manually at times, creating endless mocks for testing, or wrapping legacy completion handlers to work with `async` code.

With **Swift 5.9**, Apple has given the developer community the keys to the compiler itself. **Swift Macros** represent one of the biggest shifts in Swift metaprogramming so far. They aren't just a convenience feature; they change how libraries and architecture patterns can be expressed with less boilerplate.

What are Macros?

At its core, a macro is a compile-time transformation that can be invoked either as an attribute (attached macros) or as an expression (freestanding macros) to generate Swift code.

When the compiler encounters a macro invocation, it expands it during compilation by running the macro implementation (provided by a compiler plugin). The macro inspects the relevant syntax, generates new Swift code, and the compiler then compiles the expanded result alongside your original source.

To understand why this is revolutionary, compare it with the tools you used before: `Mirror` and `@resultBuilder`.

Macros vs. Mirror

You used `Mirror` to dynamically inspect a type's properties (e.g., for JSON parsing or logging).

- **The Problem**: `Mirror` operates at runtime. It can be slow, it hides structure from the compiler, and failures tend to show up late, as missing keys, unexpected shapes, or type mismatches during execution rather than at build time.
- **The Macro Solution**: Macros run at compile time. They can generate code before the app runs, which means no runtime reflection cost, and errors surface as build failures instead of production surprises.

Macros vs. @resultBuilder

Result builders (introduced in SwiftUI) enable transforming a sequence of statements into a single value.

- **The Limitation**: Result builders transform a block of statements into a single value within that expression context. They don't create new declarations (types, methods, conformances), and they don't perform general-purpose structural code generation.

- **The Macro Solution**: Macros leverage the `SwiftSyntax` library, which has access to the Abstract Syntax Tree (AST). They can read variable names, function types, and access levels of structs, then generate new declarations based on that data.

Type 1: Freestanding Macros

The first type of macro is a **Freestanding Macro**. They appear in your code as expressions that start with a hash symbol (#). They behave somewhat like functions, but instead of being executed at runtime, they expand at compile time into ordinary Swift expressions that may produce runtime values.

Freestanding macros are unique because they do not attach to a specific declaration, such as a struct or class; they stand alone within the code flow.

The Problem: Runtime Validation

Consider the common task of creating a URL from a string.

```
// The old way
let url = URL(string: "https://www.apple.com")!
```

You often use force-unwrapping because you know the string is static and correct. However, the compiler does not know that. It requires you to handle an optional that you believe won't be nil, risking a crash.

The Solution: The #URL Macro

A freestanding macro can validate the string during compilation.

```
// For illustration, imagine a #URL macro:
let url = #URL("https://www.apple.com")
```

How it works:

1. **Analysis**: The macro reads the string literal "https://www.apple.com".

2. **Validation**: It verifies whether this string is a correctly formatted URL.

- If it is **invalid** (e.g., `#URL("http :// bad")`), the macro produces a compile-time error, causing the build to fail. You can't ship a bug.

- If it is **valid**, the macro expands into a `URL`-producing expression (often equivalent to `URL(string: "https://www.apple.com")`, but guaranteed by compile-time validation).

3. **Result**: You obtain the safety of a non-optional type, with confidence that the URL is correctly formed.

Type 2: Attached Macros

Another powerful category of macros is attached macros. These are identified by the @ symbol (e.g., `@Observable`, and `@Model` from SwiftData).

Attached macros don't replace your source; they augment it. They attach to declarations (types, members, functions, variables) and can generate additional code —such as new members or synthesized conformances—within the appropriate scope.

The Problem: Legacy Boilerplate

A significant challenge in modern iOS development is bridging the gap between legacy callback-based APIs and modern Swift Concurrency (`async/await`).

Imagine you have a legacy networking service:

```
class NetworkService {
  func fetchUserProfile(id: String, completion: @escaping
(Result<User, Error>) -> Void) {
    // complex legacy networking logic...
  }
}
```

To use this with `async/await`, you need to write a wrapper using `withCheckedContinuation` manually. This process is tedious, error-prone, and repetitive.

The Solution: The @GenerateAsync Macro

You can create an attached macro called `@GenerateAsync`. When attached to a function, it analyzes the function signature, detects the completion handler, and automatically generates the async version.

```
class NetworkService {
  @GenerateAsync
  func fetchUserProfile(id: String, completion: @escaping
(Result<User, Error>) -> Void) {
    // legacy logic
  }
}
```

Macro Expansion (Generated Code): This macro automatically creates a "peer" function in the background.

```
// Generated by @GenerateAsync
extension NetworkService {
  func fetchUserProfile(id: String) async throws -> User {
    return try await withCheckedThrowingContinuation
{ continuation in
      self.fetchUserProfile(id: id) { result in
        continuation.resume(with: result)
      }
    }
  }
}
```

You never need to write the continuation logic. If the original function's signature changes, the macro automatically updates the async version the next time you build.

Why Macros are a Game-Changer

Swift Macros are more than just a convenience; they represent a fundamental shift in how Swift libraries can be designed.

The End of Boilerplate

The primary goal for developers is to write business logic, not boilerplate code. Macros address the *boilerplate problem* by allowing library creators to write foundational code once and have it automatically replicated by the compiler. From the `@Observable` macros in SwiftUI to SwiftData's `@Model`, Apple already demonstrates that macros are becoming the standard for reducing code verbosity.

Consistency and Safety

Humans tend to make mistakes and copy-and-paste errors; compilers do not. When you manually conform to `Codable` or `Equatable` for complex types, you might overlook a property. A well-written macro won't overlook a property, and it can enforce that generated code stays aligned with the source declaration.

White Box Magic

Historically, code-generation tools in iOS were opaque: you ran a script, and a file appeared. Swift macros are now integrated into Xcode. You can right-click a macro and select "Expand Macro" to see exactly what code is being generated. This transparency builds trust; you're not relying on magic. Instead, you rely on code that you can see, debug, and understand.

Swift Macros shift complexity from the application layer to the compiler layer, often resulting in codebases that are safer, faster, and easier to read.

Key Points

- Metaprogramming is a technique for writing code that creates, examines, or modifies other code, rather than just executing application logic.
- Metaprogramming is the best way to eliminate boilerplate, reduce copy-paste mistakes, and create a single source of truth for repetitive logic.
- `Mirror` enables a program to examine its own structure (properties, types, and values) during execution.
- You create a `Mirror(reflecting: instance)` to access the `children` property, which allows you to iterate over labels and values dynamically.
- `Mirror` enables the creation of generic tools, such as a recursive `prettyPrint` function, that can handle any type without knowing its structure in advance.
- Reflection in Swift is read-only (you cannot modify values) and is computationally expensive; it should be avoided in performance-critical loops.
- `@dynamicMemberLookup` lets you access properties with dot syntax (for example, `object.name`), even if those properties aren't available at compile time. The compiler converts dot-syntax calls into a specific subscript call: `subscript(dynamicMember: String)`. It bridges the gap between Swift's strict type safety and dynamic data, making it ideal for creating clean wrappers around JSON, dictionaries, or scripts.
- `@resultBuilder` powers SwiftUI by allowing the creation of Domain-Specific Languages (DSLs) where code specifies what to do, not how to do it. This attribute converts a sequence of distinct statements (such as a list of Views) into a single combined value.
- Every result builder must implement `static func buildBlock(…)`, which specifies how components are combined.
- To support logic like `if` and `else` within a DSL, the builder must implement methods such as `buildOptional` and `buildEither`.
- Introduced in **Swift 5.9**, **Macros** run at compile time to create and insert new code into your source files, with no runtime reflection cost.
- Unlike result builders, **Macros** interact with the Abstract Syntax Tree through **SwiftSyntax**, enabling them to examine types in detail and create entirely new declarations.

- Freestanding macros stand alone (like `#URL`) and act as expressions that return a value or perform validation, effectively replacing runtime crashes with compile-time errors.
- Attached macros are applied to declarations (like `@GenerateAsync`) and enhance code by adding new methods, properties, or conformances to existing types.

Where to Go From Here?

You have now stepped behind the curtain of the Swift language. Having been introduced to metaprogramming, you've progressed from simply using Apple's tools to building your own. You understand that `Mirror` provides visibility during runtime inspection, `@resultBuilder` helps you create expressive DSLs, and **Swift Macros** enable code generation during compilation.

But power comes with responsibility. The risk of metaprogramming is over-engineering. Just because you can use a macro to generate a single line doesn't mean you should.

Your next step is to think about what you've learned so far. Review your current project and identify the code you write repeatedly. Is it JSON parsing or mock data for tests? These are great options for macros. Also, consider replacing a complex configuration pattern in your app with a `@resultBuilder` to make the call site clearer.

If you're serious about macros, explore the `swiftlang/swift-syntax` repository from GitHub, review the examples, and try creating a macro or two on your own.

Metaprogramming isn't just a coding technique; it's a way of thinking about how you build software. It encourages you to focus on the structure of your code rather than just the logic. As you grow, use the tools available to make your code cleaner, safer, and more expressive for everyone working with it.

If you feel tempted to write boilerplate code, remember the words of a wise man:

```
"Why waste time say lot word when few word do trick?"
```

Chapter 8: Architectural Dynamics: Modularization & Linking

Aaqib Hussain

The word **Architecture** derives from *Greek* roots, combining *Arkhi* (" Chief" or "Principal") and *Tekton* ("Builder" or "Craftsman"). As the architect of an app, your responsibility is to be the principal builder. You must construct a system that is not only scalable and stable, but also resilient to change. Authentic architecture isn't just about how you write code inside a function; it is about how you organize that code across the entire system.

Why does this organization matter to you? Structuring your app into loosely coupled components provides three critical advantages:

1. **Maintainability**: You isolate features so that changes in one area do not break another.

2. **Velocity**: You enable parallel development, allowing large teams to work simultaneously without getting in each other's way.

3. **Performance**: You optimize the build system to drastically reduce compilation times.

This is where modularization becomes your structural reinforcement. It transforms a monolithic, fragile codebase into a structured assembly of reusable parts. It elevates boundaries, encourages clean interfaces, and, as a significant side effect, accelerates your feedback loops.

In this final chapter, you will dissect the mechanics of software architecture. You will examine the differences between static and dynamic linking, master the Swift Package Manager ecosystem, and explore the physics of the build graph to engineer apps that scale effortlessly.

The Case for Modularization

Most iOS apps and projects initially start with a monolithic architecture, using a single Xcode target that contains all source files, resources, and configurations. In the early stages, this setup is efficient when the project is small and still evolving. It's easy to add new files, and `CMD + R` is instant.

However, as your codebase grows, the monolith becomes a liability. Compile times increase from seconds to minutes because even a minor change can trigger a complete rebuild of the project. At this moment, the project reaches a point where you have enough time to brew a coffee, drink it, and contemplate why you didn't become a carpenter instead. Merge conflicts become more common as teams expand, often centered on the `project.pbxproj` file.

Modularization involves transforming this liability into an asset by splitting up the large single target into smaller, independent modules. Each of these targets produces its own binary. To do this effectively, you need to understand the structure of the graph you're building.

Breaking the Monolith

When you split a monolithic app, you're essentially trading convenience for control. By isolating code into modules, you enforce the **Separation of Concerns** at the compiler level.

With a monolithic app, boundaries are ill-defined. Nothing prevents a View Controller from accessing a Networking Manager and modifying a public property. In a modularized app, these boundaries are physical. If the Networking module doesn't explicitly mark a property as `public`, the UI layer cannot simply see it. This strict enforcement prevents *spaghetti code* better than any code review could.

However, the immediate benefit you will notice is **Incremental Compilation**. When you modify a specific file inside a module, Xcode only needs to recompile that module and the targets that depend on it. It doesn't need to touch other unchanged modules.

> **Note**: Incremental Compilation is a compiler strategy that compiles only the parts of the code that have changed.

The Dependency Graph

Once you're working with modules, you're not just creating modules but also managing a **Directed Acyclic Graph (DAG)**, possibly without realizing it.

- **Directed**: Dependency flows in one direction. For example, Module A imports Module B.
- **Acyclic**: There are no cycles.

The compiler relies on this graph to determine the build order. If Module A depends on Module B, then Module B must be compiled and linked before Module A can even start.

The main problem in modular architecture is **Circular Dependency**. Imagine the **Profile** module needs to know about the **Settings** module to save preferences, but the **Settings** module needs to display the current user's avatar.

- Profile module imports the settings module.
- Settings module imports the profile module.

The compiler faces a contradiction: it cannot build Profile until Settings is finished, but it cannot finish building Settings until Profile is built. It is the architectural equivalent of two people stuck in a revolving door. Neither can move forward until the other one leaves, but neither is willing to step out. Xcode will show a cryptic build error indicating a dependency cycle.

To fix this, think like an architect and apply the **Dependency Inversion Principle**.

1. Create a third module, **UserPreferences**.
2. Define a protocol inside it.
3. Have both Profile and Settings modules import it.

Now, both high-level modules depend on low-level definitions, breaking the cycle and restoring the **DAG**.

Libraries vs. Modules vs. Frameworks

When discussing modularization, developers often use the terms "Framework," "Library," and "Modules" interchangeably. As an advanced Swift developer, you should be able to distinguish between them because they represent different stages of the build process.

The Library (.a or .dylib)

The library is the compiled code that serves as the module's core. It contains the machine code derived from your Swift source. It can be of two types:

1. **Static Library**: An archive of object files. It's essentially a zip of compiled code that gets merged directly into your app's binary executable.
2. **Dynamic Library**: A standalone binary that loads into memory during runtime.

The Module (.swiftmodule)

The library contains executable code, but it doesn't tell the Swift compiler how to use it. In languages such as C or Objective-C, header files (`.h`) define the public interface. In Swift, the compiler creates a **Module Map** (`.modulemap` file, which connects C/Objective-C headers with Swift's module system) and a `.swiftmodule` file.

- The `.swiftmodule` file is a binary format that contains the Swift module metadata, representing your public types, generic constraints, and function signatures.
- When you write `import Profile`, the compiler searches for `Profile.swiftmodule` to perform type checking. It does not look at the `.a` or `.dylib` files at this stage; that occurs later during the linking phase.

The Framework (.framework)

A framework is not a file type; it's a package, specifically a directory with a known structure. It bundles the **Library** (the code) together with the **Module** (the interface) and **Resources** (images, storyboards, localization strings, and so on).

Apple operating system utilize frameworks because they provide a single, portable, self-contained unit that includes everything a user needs to use your code.

Component	Extension	Role
Library	.a / .dylib	The compiled machine code (Runtime).
Module	.swiftmodule	The public interface definitions (Compile-time).
Framework	.framework	The container holding the library, module, and resources.

Library vs. Module vs. Framework

Grasping this difference is essential when you're trying to debug "module not found" errors. Usually, it means that the compiler found the framework folder but cannot locate the `.swiftmodule` file because it is missing or incompatible with your Swift version.

Static vs. Dynamic Linking

The **Linking** process begins as soon as the compiler successfully generates the object files (`.o`) from your source code.

The linker combines all object files, including those from your imported frameworks, into a single executable. It resolves symbols (variables and functions) and ensures the CPU knows exactly which memory address to jump to when a module calls a function in another module.

There are fundamentally two ways in which linking can occur: **Static linking** and **Dynamic linking**. Understanding the difference is not only important academically, but it's the primary factor in your app's startup and build performance.

Static Linking (.a)

When you link the library statically, the linker effectively "copies and pastes" the compiled object code from the library's archive (`.a`) into your app's main executable binary. Once the build is finished, the library effectively ceases to exist as an independent entity. It physically becomes part of your app.

The linker scans your code to identify which symbols are used. It then extracts the relevant object files from the static library and rewrites the memory addresses to place the library code inline with your app code.

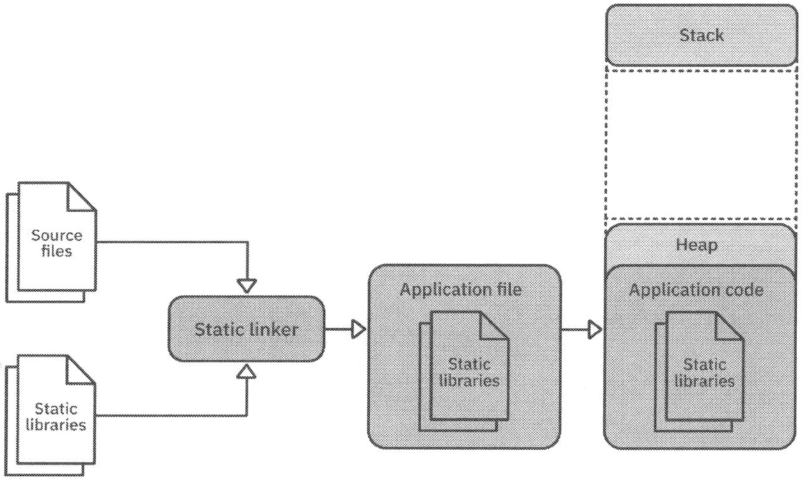

A figure representing Static Linking.

The Pros

- **App Launch Speed**: Because the code is already in the main binary, the OS doesn't need to look for it, load it, or verify the signature during launch. The code is ready to execute immediately.
- **Compiler Optimization**: Static Linking enables **Link-Time Optimization (LTO)**. Because the compiler can see the entire codebase as a single unit, it can perform aggressive optimizations, such as inlining functions that are often impossible across dynamic boundaries.
- **Dead Code Stripping**: The linker is smart. If your library contains 50 helper functions but you only use one, the linker usually discards the remaining 49. This is the default behavior for release builds. This helps maintain a lean and compact binary.

The Cons and Some Surprises

- **Binary Size Duplication**: Consider an app and an extension that are both linked to a networking library. The networking library is copied twice, once in the app and again in the extension binary.
- **Slow Clean Builds**: During development, every time you clean and rebuild the app, each target that statically links the library performs its own linking steps, which slows down the overall build time.
- **Ghost Code**: Just because you put code into a static library doesn't mean it will actually end up in your final app. If you have special code, such as an Obj-C category or a function marked with `__attribute__((used))`, that isn't explicitly called by name, the linker may ignore the whole file, and the code will be missing from your app.
- **Duplicate Conflicts**: If a static library is incorporated into multiple frameworks, and those frameworks are used in the app, you'll commonly see runtime issues due to multiple definitions of the same class.
- **Missing Symbols**: This can hide many static library issues. For example, if you forget to include the function your library refers to, the linker stops and reports an error. If dead code stripping is enabled and the linker decides that the path to that missing function is never executed by your app, it simply deletes the reference and stays silent. You won't know the code is missing until the app tries to use it later and crashes.

Dynamic Linking (.dylib / .framework)

With dynamic linking, the static linker places a *promise* (a stub) in your executable. The promise says: *"I don't have the code for this function, but you can find it in* FrameworkB.framework *at runtime."*

The actual code remains in a separate binary (`.dylib`). It is loaded into memory only when the user launches the app.

When the user taps your app icon, the kernel spawns your process. Before the process reaches `main()`, the dynamic linker `dyld` runs.

The dynamic linker finds all the dynamic frameworks your app lists as dependencies, then maps them into the process's memory space. Finally, it fulfills all those *promises* in your code, replacing the stubs with actual memory addresses where the dynamic libraries were loaded.

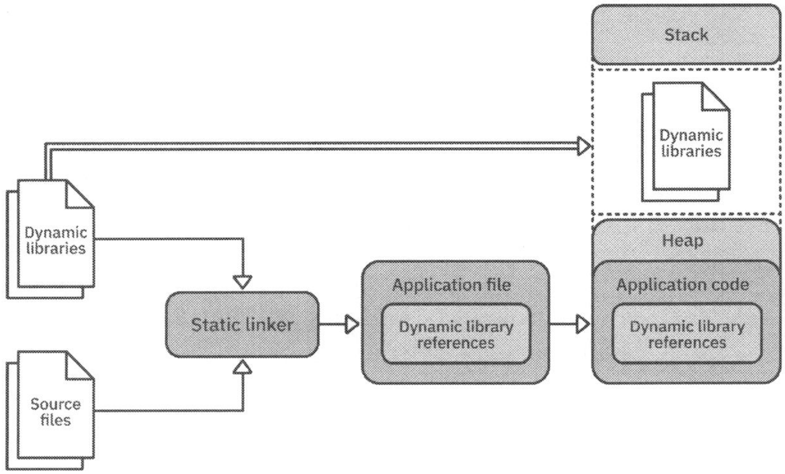

How the process of Dynamic Linking occurs.

You can also inspect the dyld linking process using the `dyld_usage` tool. In your terminal, run:

```
sudo dyld_usage <name-of-your-app>
```

Then launch your app. You will see a long list of logs; look for an entry like this:

```
12:23:59.242875   app launch -> 0x100db0000
6.512988 YourAppName.33688106
```

In addition to using Instruments, this command lets you verify app launch time and examine the dynamic linking process.

The Pros

- **Fast Incremental Builds**: If you have a bunch of dynamic frameworks and change a line of code in one of them, Xcode only needs to recompile and relink that specific framework. The main app binary doesn't need to be modified; it simply points to the new reference.
- **Memory Sharing**: System frameworks (like `UIKit` or `SwiftUI`) are dynamic. The OS loads them into memory once and shares them across all running apps. This saves a massive amount of RAM.

The Cons

- **Slow App Launch**: This is one of the primary downsides of dynamic frameworks. Each dynamic framework you add increases the pre-main time because the dynamic linker must perform extensive work before your app can even display its launch screen. Apple recommends keeping the number of dynamic frameworks to a minimum.

- **No Aggressive Stripping**: Because a library is a standalone binary, it must contain all its public code in case the app needs it. As a result, unused symbols are harder to strip from a dynamic library.

The Decision Matrix

So, as an app architect, which one do you choose?

By default, when using Swift Package Manager (SPM), the target is usually **static**. However, you can override this by explicitly declaring `.dynamic` in your `Package.swift`, but you should have a solid reason to do so.

Use the following matrix to guide your linking strategy:

Scenario	Recommendation	Why?
Feature Modules (e.g., `Profile`, `Cart`)	Static	Optimizes launch time. Features are typically used only by the main app.
Core Utilities (e.g., `Networking`, `DesignSystem`) used only by the App	Static	Enables the compiler to inline small helper functions for maximum performance.
Shared Code (App + Widget + Notification Extension)	Dynamic	Prevents code duplication. If you link statically here, the same heavy logic is bloated across three different executables in your bundle.
Large Pre-compiled Vendor SDKs	Dynamic	Often distributed as XCFrameworks. Keeping them dynamic prevents them from slowing down your daily link times during development.

Choosing Between Static & Dynamic Frameworks

The Rule of Thumb: For performance, the default approach is **Static Linking**. Use **Dynamic** when you need to share code between extensions or when you are explicitly optimizing for incremental build speeds in a large codebase.

The Swift Package Manager (SPM) Ecosystem

For many years, developers have relied on third-party tools like **Carthage** and **CocoaPods** to manage external dependencies. These tools were essentially workarounds layered on top of Xcode project files (`.xcodeproj`).

The SPM is different; it's integrated directly into the build system. More importantly, it's defined in Swift. This makes your build configuration type-safe, compiled, and logic-capable.

To master modularization, you must stop treating `Package.swift` as a simple config file and start treating it as a blueprint for your architecture.

Deconstructing Package.swift

A `Package.swift` file is the manifest that defines a package's dependency graph. It has three core components: **Products**, **Targets**, and **Settings**.

1. Products vs. Targets

New architects often confuse these two.

- **Targets** are the basic building blocks. They contain the source code.
- **Products** are the executable artifacts (libraries or executables) that you expose to clients.

You can have internal targets that are not exposed as products at all. For example, you might have a `CoreNetworking` target and a `CoreNetworkingTesting` target. You expose `CoreNetworking` to the outside, but you keep the testing internal to your package unless you explicitly create a product for it.

2. Resources and Bundles

Handling assets in modular code is a bit trickier than in a monolith. You cannot just call `Bundle.main`.

When you add resources (images, JSON, storyboards) to a target, SPM synthesizes a new Bundle for that module.

- `.process`: The default. It optimizes platform resources (compiles asset catalogs, compresses images).

- `.copy`: Preserves the directory structure exactly as is.

To access these resources, you must use the compiler-synthesized accessor `Bundle.module`. If you try to use `Bundle(for: MyClass.self)`, you might accidentally grab the wrong bundle if the linking type (static vs dynamic) changes.

3. Conditional Build Settings

You often need to pass flags to the compiler. SPM allows this via `swiftSettings`.

```
targets: [
  .target(
    name: "MyFeature",
    swiftSettings: [
      .define("DEBUG_NETWORK", .when(configuration: .debug)),
      .enableExperimentalFeature("StrictConcurrency")
    ]
  )
]
```

This is how you enforce strictness or enable experimental features on a per-module basis.

Local Packages & The Monorepo

One of the most effective ways to use SPM is the Monorepo approach.

Instead of creating hundreds of repositories for each of your packages, which ultimately creates a versioning nightmare, you put them all in the same repository as your main app.

The Setup:

1. Create a folder named `Packages/` in your root directory.
2. Initialize new packages inside that folder (`swift package init`).
3. In your workspace, drag the folder into Xcode.

Finally, in your main app's dependencies or in a *"umbrella"* package, you reference these modules using a **file path**, not a **URL**.

```
dependencies: [
  // No version requirement needed!
  .package(path: "../Packages/ProfileFeature"),
  .package(path: "../Packages/CoreUI")
]
```

Benefits:

- You edit a file in `ProfileFeature`, hit Run, and the app updates. No `git add`, `git push`, `git tag`, or SPM Update required.
- Code searching finds everything. The refactoring tools work across module boundaries.

Binary Targets (XCFrameworks)

Sometimes, you cannot (or should not) ship source code.

- **Vendor SDKs**: You're distributing a proprietary feature or algorithm.
- **Build Time Optimization**: You have a massive module (like OpenCV or a custom 3D engine) that takes 5 minutes to compile. You should compile it once and let the team use the binary.

XCFramework is the right tool for that.

An **XCFramework** is a bundle that contains multiple compiled binaries for different architectures, for example, `ios-arm64` for devices and `ios-arm64_x86_64-simulator` for the simulator.

Declaring the Target: In your `Package.swift`, you define a `binaryTarget`.

```
targets: [
  .binaryTarget(
    name: "MySecretAlgo",
    // Local file
    path: "Binaries/MySecretAlgo.xcframework"
  )
]
```

When the compiler encounters a `binaryTarget`, it skips the compilation phase for that framework and proceeds directly to linking. This is a powerful optimization technique for stabilizing build times in large teams.

Versioning and Distribution Strategies

Writing a module is one thing, and maintaining it for others is another. When you distribute a framework, whether to the open-source community or to another team in your company, you're essentially establishing a contract.

The build system relies on this contract to resolve the dependency graph. If you break the contract, you break the build.

Semantic Versioning (SemVer)

SPM relies heavily on Semantic Versioning to make decisions. It's not just a numbering scheme but a language that tells the resolver how safe it is to upgrade.

Format: `major.minor.patch` (e.g., `1.4.2`)

- `major`: You made incompatible API changes. (Code that compiled previously may no longer compile.)
- `minor`: You added functionality in a backward-compatible way.
- `patch`: You made backward-compatible bug fixes.

When you define a dependency in your `Package.swift`, you typically specify the version with `.upToNextMajor(from: "1.0.0")`. This tells the resolver: *"I accept any version from 1.0.0 up to (but not including) 2.0.0."*

This is why complying with SemVer is critical. For example, if you introduce a breaking change (renaming a public function) in your framework and only increment the *minor* version (e.g., `1.1.0` to `1.2.0`), you'll end up breaking the build for every consumer who trusted your SemVer promise.

> **Note:** `Package.resolved` is generated (or updated) every time SPM performs dependency resolution. It records the exact versions of all resolved Swift package dependencies to ensure reproducible builds across machines.

Dependency Hell: The Diamond Problem

Imagine the following scenario:

- **Module A** depends on **Logger v1.0**.
- **Module B** depends on **Logger v2.0** (which has a breaking change).
- Your app imports both **Module A** and **Module B**.

Basically, if Dante had been an iOS developer, he would have added a Tenth Circle to the Inferno specifically for this. The build system now gets stuck. It cannot build the app with two different versions of the `Logger` framework in the same executable.

Unlike the web ecosystem (e.g., Node.js/NPM), which allows nested dependencies (each module receives its own copy), Swift/iOS enforces a flat namespace. In a single process, there can be only one implementation of a symbol. `Logger.log()` cannot mean two different things simultaneously.

The Resolution: SPM resolves dependencies by selecting a single package version that satisfies all the declared version constraints. When multiple versions are valid, it prefers the latest one within the overlapping range defined by the constraints. If no overlapping version exists, dependency resolution fails.

The Fix: As an architect, you must coordinate updates across your team. This is why monorepos are popular: they require all modules to use the same versions of dependencies, eliminating version conflicts.

API Design for Modules

Controlling what is visible to the outside world is fundamental to compile-time performance and long-term stability.

1. `public` vs. `open`

- `public`: A consumer can call this class or method, but cannot override or subclass it. This allows the compiler to make stronger optimization assumptions.
- `open`: A consumer can override and subclass it. This is the most expensive access level because it requires the compiler to use dynamic dispatch for all operations, thereby preventing many optimizations.

2. The `package` Access Control

For years, Swift developers struggled with a limitation: if you wanted to share code between two targets in the same package (e.g., Core and UI), you had to make it `public`. However, that also exposed it to the rest of the world.

There is another access control in Swift: `package`.

- `internal`: Visible only within the target.
- `package`: Visible to any target in the same package (but hidden from external consumers).
- `public`: Visible to everyone.

This changes the game for modularization. It allows you to create Swift packages with shared internal utilities that remain invisible to the client app.

3. `@inlinable`

This attribute is a double-edged sword. When you mark a function with `@inlinable`, you allow the compiler to copy the function's body directly into the client's code during compilation.

- **Pros**: Can deliver significant performance gains, especially for tight loops (`Array.map`). It avoids the overhead of a function call.
- **Cons**: Your implementation details are exposed. If you change the logic of an `@inlinable` function in a future release, consumers will not see the change until they recompile their own code, because the old logic was already baked into their binary.

Use `@inlinable` only for small, stable algorithms that are unlikely to change over time. Never use it for logic that depends on private state.

Build Time Optimization

In professional software development, build time is *currency*. If a clean build takes 20 minutes and an incremental build takes 2 minutes, a developer who builds 30 times a day loses an hour of concentration and efficiency every day.

As an architect, optimizing build times isn't simply about making builds *fast*; it's about structuring your dependency graph so the compiler does only the work necessary.

Compiler Flags: Hunting for Slow Code

Sometimes, the *slowdown* isn't just the architecture but the code itself. Swift has a powerful type inference engine, but complex expressions (especially those involving nested closures, generics, or overloaded operators) can cause the type checker to take exponential time to resolve.

You can ask the Swift compiler to tell you exactly which functions are slowing down compilation by passing specific arguments to the frontend.

In your Target's **Build Settings** -> **Other Swift Flags**, add:

- `-Xfrontend -warn-long-function-bodies=100` This triggers a warning for any function that takes longer than 100ms to compile.

- `-Xfrontend -warn-long-expression-type-checking=100` This triggers a warning for each particular expression (such as a complex dictionary literal or a chained `map/filter`) that takes longer than 100ms to type-check.

This is how the setup looks in the **Build Settings**:

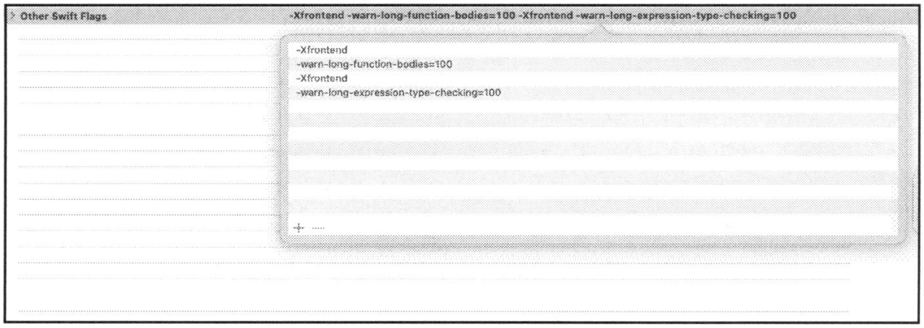

Setting up Other Swift Flags

Frequent Causes:

- **Collection Literals**: Large dictionaries or arrays missing explicit type annotations (`let data: [String: Any] = ...`).
- **Operator Overloading**: Chaining + on strings or custom math operators.
- **SwiftUI Bodies**: Deeply nested view builders can sometimes overwhelm the compiler. Breaking complex views into smaller subviews often significantly speeds up compilation.

Indexing & The Index Store

While compilation builds the binary, indexing builds the brain.

The **Index Store** is the database that lives inside your `Derived Data` folder. From it, Xcode gains the power of features such as *jump to definition*, *Find Callers*, and refactoring tools.

The indexing process runs separately from the build process, but they share the same CPU resources.

- **The Hang**: If you see "Indexing..." stuck at the top of Xcode indefinitely, or if autocomplete stops working, it likely means that your Index Store is corrupted.

- **The Fix**: You don't always need to "Clean Build Folder" (which deletes the binaries). You can clear only the index:

1. Navigate to `DerivedData/YourApp/Index`
2. Delete the `DataStore` folder.
3. Restart Xcode.

Xcode will rebuild the index from scratch without forcing a full recompile of your binaries.

Explicit Modules: Apple is pushing towards **explicit modules**, where the build system separates the *scanning* phase (finding dependencies) from the *building* phase (builds the modules first and then the source code). This prevents the compiler from repeatedly parsing the same headers across targets, drastically reducing overhead in highly modularized setups. This is the default behavior in Xcode 26 and later, and it relies heavily on an acyclic dependency graph.

Key Points

- True architecture isn't just about code quality; it is about system organization. It aims to maintain usability, velocity, and performance.
- Monolithic apps suffer from slow compilation times, frequent merge conflicts, and blurred feature boundaries.
- Modularization enables the compiler to rebuild only the parts of the app that changed, significantly accelerating development cycles.
- You are building a **Directed Acyclic Graph (DAG)**. Circular dependencies break the graph and must be resolved using the **Dependency Inversion Principle**.
- A **Library** is the compiled code (`.a`/`.dylib`), a **Module** is the interface definition (`.swiftmodule`, containing the AST/SIL), and a **Framework** is the package container (`.framework`).
- Static linking copies code into the executable, optimizing launch time and enabling aggressive optimizations at the cost of slower clean builds.
- Dynamic linking references code at runtime via `dyld`, enabling memory sharing and faster incremental builds at the cost of slower app launches.

- Default to **Static** for feature modules and core utilities. Use **Dynamic** only when sharing code between extensions or optimizing build times at scale.
- In modules, use the compiler-synthesized property `Bundle.module` to access resources regardless of linking style.
- Develop local packages within the same repository using **file path** `(path: "../Packages/ProfileFeature")` to avoid versioning fatigue.
- Use `package` access control to share code within a component without exposing it publicly. Avoid `open` unless necessary, as dynamic dispatch incurs costs.
- Use `-warn-long-function-bodies` and `-warn-long-expression-type-checking` to identify specific code blocks that are strangling your build times.

Where to Go From Here?

You have reached the final page of the last chapter, which also brings you to the end of *The Swift Internals*, but do not mistake this for the finish line. In reality, this is just the starting line.

You began this journey by delving into the microscopic details of Memory Layout and Reference Counting. You explored the power of Generics, the complexity of Concurrency, and the magic of the compiler. Finally, you zoomed out to take a macroscopic view of Modularization and Linking.

You now understand that every abstraction has a cost. Behind every `import`, a linker is doing heavy lifting (not literally). You know that *safety* in Swift is often a choice, and sometimes you must reach toward the *unsafe* side to get the job done.

Bring this mindset into your daily work. Don't just fix bugs; understand *why* they happened. Don't just optimize build time; profile the dependency graph as well. The tools will change. Swift will evolve. But the dynamics of how software is built, linked, and executed remain the foundation of everything a software developer does.

You're no longer just a coder; you're a master of Swift. When people ask whether your modular architecture can handle the scale, look them in the eye and say: "**It can.**"

As you turn to leave, look back and say: "**You have no idea how high it can scale.**"

The foundation is set. The tools are in your hands. Now, go build something robust.

9 Conclusion

What a journey it's been! From understanding how Swift's type system shapes abstraction to exploring compiler internals, memory management, and modular architecture, you've taken a deep dive into the mechanics that power the Swift language.

By applying the concepts in this book, you'll be able to reason more clearly about how Swift behaves internally. Whether you're optimizing performance, designing scalable architectures, or debugging complex behavior, the knowledge you've gained will help you approach problems with greater confidence and clarity.

We hope this book encourages you to continue exploring the deeper layers of Swift and the systems that support modern software development. The language continues to evolve, and staying curious about how it works will always be one of the best ways to grow as a developer.

If you're interested in going even further, explore additional Swift and iOS development resources on our site. Topics like advanced SwiftUI, design patterns, concurrency, and performance optimization can help deepen the understanding you began building here.

If you have any questions or comments as you work through this book, please stop by our forums at https://forums.kodeco.com and look for the particular forum category for this book.

Thank you again for purchasing this book. Your continued support is what makes the books, tutorials, videos and other things we do at Kodeco possible. We truly appreciate it!

– The *Swift Internals* team

Made in United States
Orlando, FL
04 November 2026

90201155R00120